GOLF

HEAVEN'S GAME ON EARTH

LEARNING GOLF MECHANICS FROM
KINGDOM PRINCIPLES

CHUCK HAMMETT

Foreword by David Gossett, PGA Tour Champion

D1509743

SELAH PRESS
PUBLISHING

Golf, Heaven's Game on Earth: Learning golf mechanics from Kingdom principles

Copyright © 2019 Chuck Hammett

ISBN: 978-0-578-50356-1

Printed in The United States of America
Published by Selah Press, LLC, selah-press.com
Editor, Venessa Knizley
Golf Images: Adam Sanner Photography
Gold Graphic Design: Christine Dupre
Cover Design: Christine Dupre

Style: Editorial liberties have been taken for emphasis. Names of God and references to Him are capitalized.

Unless otherwise noted, Scripture quotations are taken from the New King James Version. Copyright © 1979, 1980, 1982 by Thomas Nelson, Inc. Used by permission. All rights reserved.

Notice of Rights: All rights reserved. No part of this book may be reproduced or transmitted in any form by any means, electronic, mechanical, photocopy, recording or other without the prior written permission of the publisher.

Permission: For information on getting permission for reprints and excerpts, contact: dominionmarketing@comcast.net

Notice of Liability: The author has made every effort to check and ensure the accuracy of the information presented in this book. However, the information herein is sold without warranty, either expressed or implied. Neither the author, publisher, nor any dealer or distributor of this book will be held liable for any damages caused either directly or indirectly by the instructions and information contained in this book.

Disclaimer: The author and publisher are not engaged in rendering legal services. Every effort has been made to provide the most up-to-date and accurate information possible. Technological changes may occur at any time after the publication of this book. This book may contain typographical and content errors; therefore this is only designed as a guide and resource.

Copyright: In accordance with the U.S. Copyright Act of 1976, the scanning, uploading, and electronic sharing of any part of this book without the permission of the publisher is unlawful piracy and theft of the author's intellectual property. If you would like to use material from this book (other than for review purposes), prior written permission must be obtained by contacting the publisher at info@selah-press.com. Thank you for your support of the author's rights.

Contents

Foreword by David Gossett

For me, golf became a passion at roughly ten years of age. Tournament golf became an arena to test and push myself at a game I was learning to love immensely. After numerous years of playing team sports, I decided to focus solely on golf by age fifteen. I began playing in more golf tournaments around our great country and occasionally abroad. I always appreciated how golf allows you to connect with people through time spent outdoors and during competition. While playing a game that cannot be mastered is demoralizing at times, it often draws out a desire to play more and improve.

In Chuck's book, he relates the mechanics of the golf swing to the Christian walk. Golf has provided me with numerous experiences and successes that I am grateful for. In 1997, I was the top junior in the country and the American Junior Golf Association's Player of the Year. I achieved the highest standard in amateur golf by winning the 1999 US Amateur at Pebble Beach and representing the USA in the 1999 Walker Cup. In 2000, I shot a 13 under par round of 59 in PGA Tour's final stage of qualifying school. Finally, I won a PGA Tour event in 2001 at the John Deere Classic.

Many of these were dreams of mine growing up. I am so thankful that I had the support systems, coaching, and ability to realize these dreams. When I won the US Amateur and PGA Tour event, I relied on my relationship with Christ to ground me. It helped me keep my attention on the business at hand, which was playing the game to the best of my ability. It is freeing to have a relationship with Christ and to walk by faith in dependence on Him. My relationship with Jesus allowed me to be free from focusing on results and to concentrate on competing. I would regularly write down Bible verses in my yardage book and meditate on them while walking the course. God's word helped me maintain a healthy perspective.

Despite all of my successes, golf has a funny way of humbling us all. As the years progressed in my professional career, I lost my tour card and the ability to continue playing on the PGA Tour. This was a very frustrating time in my life. However, through it all I have remained steady in knowing that my identity is in Christ, not my vocation. This requires attention to the Scripture and remembering that your worth is not performance-based, despite our society teaching us the opposite. Sound spiritual principals lead to a purposeful life.

With a relatively new career in commercial real estate and as a husband and father of four children, I know that God has a plan for me in Nashville, TN for His Kingdom. Chuck's book speaks to me personally as a call to keep my focus on the basics. For me that means trusting Jesus with the details, sticking to sound fundamentals and finding joy in the journey as I walk with God.

Many comparisons have been made between golf and life, parallel principles that bode well for a successful life and outings on the golf links, namely: integrity, honesty, humility, focus, discipline, work ethic and determination. Whether golf is a means for competition or solely a pastime, this great game brings joy, challenges and excitement.

For these reasons, I highly recommend you read Chuck Hammett's book, *Golf: Heaven's Game on Earth*. This book provides a teachable approach to many of the particulars related to the mechanics of the golf swing. It also provides a clear challenge of how to put faith into action. You will quickly notice that Chuck has a passion for golf, possesses an effective skill set for golf instruction and has a sincere heart for sharing the Gospel of Christ.

This book is a great way to learn more about the mechanics of the game. It's also a fantastic reminder to Christians that, by the power of the Holy Spirit, we can have communion with God the Father at any time, even while on the golf course and swinging a club.

I appreciate Chuck's approach in keeping a relationship with Jesus apparent when discussing golf. As a Christ follower, keeping Jesus in the forefront of my mind during everyday life can be a challenge. It is refreshing to read a work on golf that encourages me to "keep God in it." Sound mechanics set a framework from which to play the game well.

This book will help you better understand the golf swing and cultivate a blueprint for how to approach the game. Mostly, may it serve as a gracious nudge by the Holy Spirit to include the Lord in more of your everyday life...even on the golf course!

Happy swinging,
David Gossett

Introduction

Golf, Heaven's Game on Earth. What kind of a book title is that? Is there really a connection between God and the game of golf? These are good questions. I have a few thoughts on them for your consideration. I've often said that golf is Heaven's favorite sport because it's never mastered. It continues to teach you lessons. Just when you think you've figured it out or risen to a level of success in your game, your enlightenment and victory seem to fade away as quickly as they came. I've experienced the phrase, "found it, had it, lost it" many times in my golf career, usually in about a 10-minute timeframe. Golf has a way of letting you know there's always more to learn, more changes to make and more to improve upon. Perfection in the game of golf, however it's defined in your mind, is most likely never going to be achieved. So, I say again, the game of golf is never completely mastered—and I believe the greatest players of all time would quickly agree.

The true, living God of the Bible is never mastered either. He is the Master. Yet, it's important to know that the Master isn't looking to dominate or control you. He's not waiting to punish or destroy you should you make a mistake in this life. He's good, loving and kind towards you at all times. This is true, even in the challenging moments of life. He allows our choices and decisions to teach us that "doing life apart from Him doesn't work out so well." God is just and holy, yet loving in the midst of correction. God prunes for the purpose of promotion, not punishment. God is perfect. God is love. God is for you and not against you. He is a good Father.

So, what does God have to do with the game of golf and your effort to make that four foot putt on the last hole to win the club championship? Maybe a better question is, why do we separate God from golf and most things in life at all? I believe in **Acts 17:28a,** which states, *"For in Him we live and move and have our being."* I believe that we do live, move and have our being in Him. Therefore, there is opportunity for communion with the Holy Trinity, even in the midst of the movement of a golf swing. Why should we limit God's presence to a preset time in which we go to church on Sunday? If God is omnipresent, then His presence is truly everywhere. **Psalm 139: 7-10** describes this beautifully. Check it out.

Within the contents of this book, I intend to take you on a journey of abiding in the Father, Son and Holy Spirit, in the midst of learning the game of golf. Yes, I'm going to teach you solid golf mechanics that will improve your game. I will teach you foundations that you can build a sound golf swing upon. I'm very intent on you becoming a much better golfer. However, I'm more intent on you becoming the best version of yourself. This version is the one where you learn to walk closely with the Lord, being led by His Spirit down the fairways of life. This is the version where you become the "truest you," as known in the heart of the Father before time began. This is the version where you have the most fun and joy in your life, for "in your presence is fullness of joy; at your right hand are pleasures forever more." (**See Psalm 16:11)** This is the beauty of a life communing with Him. This is what you were made for. This is what He paid for.

So, open your heart and mind to "a new and living way" in your approach to the game of golf. An approach where you learn the communion between golf mechanics and kingdom principles all at the same time. Get ready to learn more about swing plane, body rotation theories, impact positions, club face release mechanisms and much more. Get ready to laugh, have fun, relax and be reminded that golf is a game to enjoy. Mostly, be prepared to encounter the love and power of God in such a way that will transform your life in a multiplicity of ways. *Golf, Heaven's Game on Earth.* Maybe it's not such a crazy title after all.

Theological Statement

As you read through this book, I'll be connecting many thoughts between the mechanics of the golf swing and biblical principles. I'll be referencing Scripture in the process. However, it's important to note that I'm not intending to take the Word of God out of context, trying to make it fit the golf principle I'm emphasizing. I believe that would be erroneous. Rather, I desire to talk about the mechanics of the golf swing in order to get you to relate to the Scripture in its proper context. I'll be building the mechanics of the swing upon the Scripture, not the Scripture upon the swing. I will be making points about golf in order to draw you closer to God; not vice versa. As already alluded to, the main purpose of this book is to train you to play the game of golf in a constant state of communion with the Living God. How is this possible, you may ask? Stay on this journey with me as you work your way through the book, and you'll be amazed at how God will speak to you through the process.

Left Handers Tribute

To all the "Lefties" out there, I apologize for the instruction in this book coming from a right-handed perspective. I actually thoroughly enjoy working with left-handed golfers, as the teachings and mechanics do mirror each other very well. You're not a second class golfer, and God loves you just as much at the "Righties." So, I honor you and believe you can implement these teachings to your swing efficiently. Here is to all of you that stand on "your side" of the golf ball.

True Story

I've been coaching the golf teams at Grace Christian Academy where my children have gone to school for several years now. At one of the banquets held at the end of the season, I was sharing the premise of this book with one of my player's dad. He listened intently with a slightly bewildered look on his face. When I finished, he paused for a few seconds to contemplate what I was sharing. His response was classic. He said, "Chuck, I have never in my whole life had one thought about God in the midst of playing golf. If anything, golf reminds me why I need a Savior." We had a good laugh over that one. Golf can definitely reveal parts of us that still need refining…If you need to find The Savior on the golf course, keep reading. You'll find Him in the pages of this book!

Chapter 1
"Foundations–The Grip"

When beginning most anything, it's important to start in a way that will afford you the greatest opportunity for success. This idea is related to "counting the costs" or laying solid foundations upon that which you can build well. Foundations are crucial to the outcome of any type of building—whether it be a physical structure, relationship, concept or even a golf swing.

I heard a story once of a common man touring through a very abstract and unique house. Part of the house was upside down; none of the walls were the same size, and rooms were built at different angles. It was supposed to represent a new form of architecture and advanced thinking. The tour guide was gloating over all the new ideas and techniques utilized in building the masterpiece. Ideas and techniques that had never been seen before. It was as if the old ways of building were now insignificant. At the end, the tour guide asked the common man for his thoughts. He simply replied, "I bet the builder didn't us an abstract method to lay the foundation." Point well made. No matter what you're building, you need a solid foundation.

There's also an order to the foundations of life that yields good things. Some are *very* good. When God created the heavens and the earth, He utilized a very specific and necessary order. Without going into a deep, theological study, here are some simple thoughts. Light. The sun and moon preceded the creation of the grasses, herbs and trees. The reason is that photosynthesis was necessary to sustain the life within them. The grasses, herbs and trees preceded the animals on land and the birds of the air so that these animals would have food to eat and a place to make their nests. The same is true of the waters being created before the sea creatures were placed into them. And man and woman were created last, in part to steward, subdue and take dominion over all that which God had created. The order was necessary to sustain life. God's foundations have a divine order to them. **(See Genesis 1)** I also believe in a proper order when building the first layers of your golf swing.

When laying the proper foundations to build a solid golf swing upon, I'm convinced you must start with the way you hold the club in your hands, simply known as the grip! In his classic book, *Five Lessons: The Modern Fundamentals of Golf*, Ben Hogan emphatically declares, "Good golf begins with a good grip." Your hands are the only part of your body that will ever have contact with the club. They have the greatest involvement in effecting the pathway of the shaft throughout the backswing and downswing. The hands manipulate the clubface angles more than anything else. They also give the most sensory feedback to your brain, with respect to the positions of the shaft and clubface in correlation to your body angles and the golf ball. When working with a student, I always look at their grip first. I can't tell you how many times I've correlated a problem with someone's swing plane back to a faulty grip. Therefore, the way you hold the club is paramount to what kind of golf swing you'll have. Let's get started.

I am going to start with a very important phrase: the handle of the golf club is held in the fingers *not* in the palms. When you open up the hands of a good golfer with a proper grip, you'll notice the fingers form a trough, through which the handle lays. You'll also notice that the handle doesn't make contact with the palms of the hands. (See photo on next page.) There are two main reasons why this is so important.

First, there will come a time in the backswing when you'll want the wrists to hinge the club. This is a tremendous source of power in the golf swing. When you hold the club in the fingers, while not guaranteed, it's much easier to achieve this hinging motion. If you hold the club in the palms, the wrists will more naturally *bow* halfway through the backswing. Many golfers feel a strain, which can be painful, in the back of their left hand. It also produces a very flat shaft angle. Ultimately, a tremendous amount of power is lost. Just by making this correction, I've seen many students gain significant distance in just a few swings.

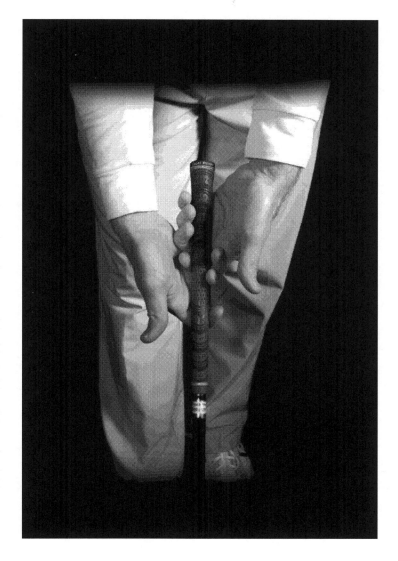

Second, there needs to be a release or "squaring" of the clubface when delivering the club through impact. When holding the club in the fingers, this release is a more natural motion. If you hold the club in the palms, especially in the left hand, the more natural delivery of the club into impact is one with an open clubface. Of course, this will make the ball fly high and to the right. Sound familiar to any of you "slicers" out there? Is it possible this grip issue is the origin of the slice? I would say yes almost every time. By gripping the club in the fingers, you may achieve some amazing results very quickly.

Therefore, starting with the left hand:

1. Place the handle of the club in the fingers. The club will pass over your wedding ring, if you wear one, and through the upper digits that are the closest to the palm. You don't want to hold the club in the tips of your fingers.
2. Wrap the fingers around the handle of the club. You'll most likely notice a slight separation in space between your trigger finger and middle fingers. This is natural, especially as it will relate to the way you place the pinky finger of your right hand on the club. More on that shortly.
3. Now let the padding of the bottom portion of your left hand, which is made up by the hypothenar muscles, fold on top of the handle. This padding is below your pinky finger. You'll feel a little pinch or pressure between these muscles and the club. As you do this, be sure to *NOT* let the handle slip out of your fingers and slide into the palm. Simply let the padding fold on top of the club.
4. Let your left thumb rest on the shaft, either straight down the middle or slightly to the right of center.

Now let's complete the grip by focusing on the right hand:

1. Let the handle rest in the fingers of your right hand. Again, not in the tips of your fingers but the upper section closest to the palm.
2. Now, let the right hand fold on top of the left thumb. The left thumb will actually disappear under the right palm. As you do

this, the hypothenar muscles of the right hand will make contact with the padding just below the left thumb. This creates a nice seal between the two hands, allowing them to work together. Don't let the contact be made on top of the left hand. Please keep it on the side just below the left thumb.

3. The right thumb will then rest on the shaft just slightly to the left of center.

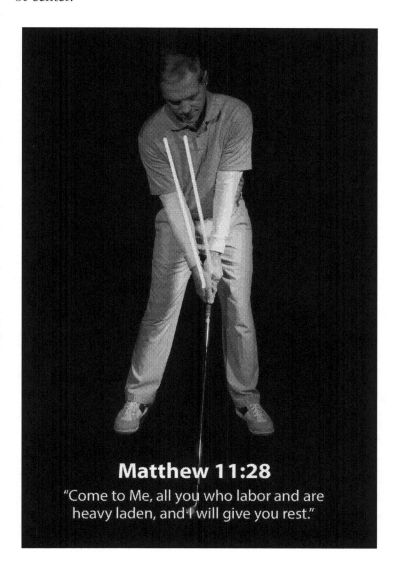

Matthew 11:28
"Come to Me, all you who labor and are heavy laden, and I will give you rest."

The two *V's* in the grip. Between the two thumbs and their respective trigger fingers, you'll notice the shape of a V between them. These V's point vertically towards your chest. (See the image on the previous page.) The vertex of the V on your left hand will point to the right of your sternum and inside your right shoulder. The V of your right hand will have a vertex that typically points in between your right shoulder and sternum. These points are not exact, but this should give you a good idea as to where they should line up. If they are pointing too far to the right, than your grip is very strong. This usually results in a closed club face in the backswing. If the vertices are pointing too far to the left, the grip is weak and will usually produce an open clubface in the backswing. Unfortunately, when clubface angles are negatively affected by a poor grip, other compensations are required to overcome them. There are always great players who are the exceptions to the rule, but you'll find that most of the professional golfers have a traditional grip. I recommend you do the same.

Matthew 11:28 shares the words of Jesus in declaring, "Come to Me, all you who labor and are heavy laden, and I will give you rest." This is a powerful Scripture that will set you free into His ways of life. Just the thought of laboring and being heavy laden in this life is unpleasant. To labor is to be fatigued or weary from a lot of hard work. To be heavy laden is to be "loaded up" or "overburdened" in ceremony. Jesus is referring to living in spiritual anxiety, due to the burden of trying to keep all of the Law of Moses. You may recall that the Ten Commandments turned into thousands of laws implemented by the Pharisees and Sadducees over time. It was impossible for the Jews to fulfill the laws perfectly. Yet, the religious mindset of the day was to continue laboring after this pursuit. This mindset is still very evident in Christians today, trying to achieve what God has already given to you freely. You're already accepted in Christ. **(See Ephesians 1:6)** It's a done deal. Settle this in your heart today. The religious mindset is exhausting and produces anxiety, as it requires a performance mentality to be acceptable to God. The religious spirit says things like, "Do it right and don't make any mistakes or else God will have to punish you. If you are not good enough God won't love you." Is Jesus against hard work and doing *things* for the Kingdom? Not at all. We were created in Christ Jesus for good works to be carried out. **Ephesians 2:10** states, "For we are His workmanship, created in Christ Jesus for good works, which God prepared beforehand that we should walk in them." However, Jesus would have us pursue these works from a place of rest in Him, not a place of work and striving. This is why He said, "I will give you rest." It's not a license to be lazy. It's a repositioning to enable you to work from rest. This isn't because you have to, but because you get to!

The key to this verse is the three words, "Come to Me." When you go to Jesus, He gives rest. It's that simple. So, as we continue to examine the golf grip, I want you to relate your grip pressure to **Matthew 11:28**. Grip pressure is a crucial item that can make or break a golf swing. I want you to relax your hands as you take hold of the club. This will allow the muscles in your arms, and up into your shoulders, to stay loose. A relaxed grip pressure aids the proper synchronization and timing throughout different parts of the swing. A tight grip pressure can easily cause a rushed release from the top of the backswing, resulting in an over-the-top shaft angle in the first move towards impact. You'll most likely lose the necessary lag in the shaft angle, which produces a great loss of power. This will make more sense as I teach on swing plane later in the book. Just trust me in this: a tight grip pressure is usually very destructive to the golf swing. It is not your friend.

Kingdom Connection Point

When placing your hands on the club, remember the "religious ceremony" that loads you up with burdens and anxiety. Know that it's determined to bury you under the lies of performance. As you take your grip, go to Jesus in your heart and soul and receive the rest that He gives. Let it manifest in your hands with a relaxed, stress free grip. Let His rest remain in your hands throughout the entire swing, all the way to your finish position. It only takes a second to implement this but has a lifetime of benefit. Hit some shots with this simple idea and see what comes of it. Let your rhythm be altered by His presence.

Chapter 2
"Foundations–The Stance"

I've been involved in the game of golf—whether as a competitor, teacher, author, lecturer or school coach—for over 40 years now. Through the years, I've been challenged at times with the following statement: "golf is not a sport." Interestingly, every time this statement has been proclaimed to me, it was made by an athlete in a different sport. They'd argue that you don't have to run in golf because the ball isn't moving, and you don't have an opponent to physically challenge yourself in the midst of the contest. I've listened to their arguments. I've given them some thoughts to consider. Ultimately, I've found that they had never really tried to play golf. I've also observed that once these athletes actually started playing golf on a consistent basis, they found out just how hard it really is. They learn that golf truly is a sport and requires a significant amount of athleticism. I've found that many of these "other athletes" quickly become hooked on golf, especially when the sport they played in their glory days fades into the distance. The fact that golf is recognized as an Olympic sport should settle the issue once and for all.

What's the point? The point is that the golf swing, because of the athleticism required, must be built upon an athletic stance. I used to give lessons to an NFL quarterback who almost won the Heisman Trophy during his college career. He was struggling with his stance— the setup position over the golf ball. I told him to get into his quarterback stance, as if he were taking a snap over the center. He naturally took that position with ease. I showed him the similarities between his football stance and the golf stance. I specified the body angles, the way his arms naturally hung and the weight distribution in his feet. I made a few minor adjustments, placed the club in his hands and he was in a solid setup position. I put him in an athletic position. He was golf ready! Let's get you in a strong golf stance as well.

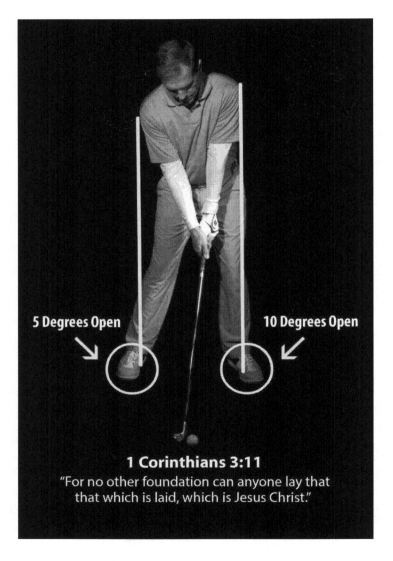

I'm going to give you a simple, systematic way to achieve the proper stance you see in the image above. First, I want you to stand tall with your hands on your hips. Your feet will be approximately shoulder width. More specifically, the in step of your feet will align to the outside of your shoulders. Your left foot will be angled out approximately 10 degrees and your right foot 5 degrees. Keep your legs totally straight, shoulders back and your chest sticking out a bit. Your hands are still on your hips. From here, I want you to tilt forward at the waist approximately 30 degrees. Please, do not let your shoulders slouch forward as you tilt. You're creating what we will refer to as your **spine angle**. Your sternum will now be in front of your toes. You'll also feel your tailbone sticking up behind you as you maintain a slight curve in your lower bank. Yes, it will feel like you're sticking your rear end out a bit.

Next, I want you to let your legs unlock, creating a slight bend in your knees. You'll create approximately 25 degrees of flex in your knees. Moving forward, I'll simply refer to this as your **knee angle.** As you're doing so, please feel the weight of your body settling into the *balls* of your feet and not on your heels. Most every sport is played on the balls of your feet, whether it be football, basketball, baseball, tennis, soccer, etc. If you try and play sports from your heels, you'll quickly find yourself out of balance and most likely getting knocked to the ground. Go ahead, get up and try it right now where you are. Remember that I am prescribing a slight bend in the knees. If you bend your knees too much, your rear end will drop, your shoulders will likely slouch forward and your weight will drop back to your heels. I have seen this pattern continuously through the years. It's not athletic and puts the golfer in a stance that is very difficult to hit a golf ball from.

Finally, I want you to let your arms come off your hips and fall forward in front of your legs. You're simply letting your arms hang naturally in front of your body due to the effect of gravity. Now, you can bring your hands together with the proper grip you learned in Chapter 1. Your hands will hang about four to five inches in front of your pant zipper, not extended out away from your body. You can also measure this distance from the butt end of your club to your zipper by using the width of your hand. This is the distance from your pinky finger to your thumb. Again, four to five inches is a good gage. The following picture will aid you visually on the stance I am describing.

Here is a quick review of the steps to take when establishing your stance:

1. Stand tall with straight legs, your hands on your hips and your chest out.

2. Tilt forward at the waist about 30 degrees with your sternum just in front of your toes.
3. Slightly flex your knees about 25 degrees with your body's weight falling into the balls of your feet.
4. Keeping your rear end high, let your arms fall in front of your body with your hands about four to five inches from your zipper.
5. Let your hands come together in the proper grip position.

If you prefer to grip the club in your hands before establishing the stance, you can do so. Simply take the club in your hands with the proper grip and extend your arms and the club straight out in front of your body. Your arms will be parallel to the ground. The club will be hinged upward with your wrists approximately 25 degrees. You can then follow the pattern previously prescribed to complete your setup. However, when you tilt forward at the waist, you'll let your arms come down in front of your body and let the club touch the ground. Once you slightly flex your knees, you'll be finished.

I also want to point out the setup height you've established in your stance over the ball. For me, personally, I stand at 5' 9". However, when I take my stance to hit a golf ball, I'm probably about 5' 5". This is what I refer to as my *setup* or *hitting height*. This is important to note, due to the fact that my clubface meets the golf ball at the ground at this height. You can determine what your setup height is on your own. I will be referring back to this later in the book, in teaching on the rotational motion of the body throughout the swing.

Congratulations! You've established a very sound setup position and grip—the true foundations of the golf swing. As you methodically repeat this process before each shot, you'll be able to build a much better swing and see results in your game. This is very important, but let's go a bit deeper. Here are some important questions that every person needs to answer: What is the foundation of life? What is eternity built upon? A clear answer is found in **1 Corinthians 3:11.** "For no other foundation can anyone lay than that which is laid, which is Jesus Christ." Jesus Christ is the foundation of all things. The foundation is the underlying support upon which the rest of the structure is built. If Jesus is not underneath all that you are building in life, than I would suggest you are building on sinking sand. **(See Matt. 7:24-27)** The house, which represents your life, probably will not stand against the storms that life will most assuredly bring. If you've lived very long, you know that the storms do come! So, what is it to truly have a foundation built upon Christ? The idea behind this foundation is to take a position in your soul that has a horizontal posture before God. In other words, it's to be laid down before Him. It's to make yourself low in a "heart stance" of reverent humility, in order to make Him high and lifted up. It's an invitation to worship. It's having a submissive mindset. This is where you make your personal mission *subordinate* to His. It's joyfully denying your own agenda so that the work of your life will be built upon the foundation of His Kingdom's advancement.

Oh, what an opportunity you now have in setting up to hit a golf ball and take your grip. In the physical realm, you're preparing to hit a superior golf shot. From your spirit, and the depths of your soul, you're exercising a moment of communion and connection with the Lord Jesus. I want you to pray into this and take the direction the Holy Spirit leads you to. You see, once you tap into Jesus as the true foundation of life, you're just scratching the surface of possible applications.

One of my favorite quotes is by T. Austin Sparks in his book, *The School of Christ.* He states, "If I should live, as long as man could ever live, I would only be on the fringe of the vast greatness of who Christ is." Let me you give you a simple, yet powerful example of how I build on the foundation of Christ. We know from **Isaiah 9:6** that Jesus is the Prince of Peace. We also know from **Colossians 1:27** that the mystery being revealed by Paul's teaching is, "Christ in you, the hope of glory." Therefore, because Christ lives in me and is the Prince of Peace, there is never a shortage of peace for any circumstance I face in life. There is never a lack of peace. I'm not stating that life is easy and without challenges. What I am saying is that in the midst of the difficulties of life, you can tap into the peace of God that surpasses your understanding of the circumstance. You can proceed forward from this peace you have in Christ. You don't have to be tossed about by your emotions.

As a Christian, peace is available always. Peace is a position in Christ. Peace is not the lack of war, loud noise or commotion. Peace is in His presence. I would suggest to you that the reason Jesus was able to sleep in the stern of the boat, in the midst of a treacherous storm, was because He lived from this place of peace. There were no storms within the realm He was living. When He spoke to the storm in the natural realm, it had to submit to the authority of peace He lived from in the Heavenly realm. **(See Matt. 4:35-41)** This same realm is available to you because you are in Him and He is in you!

Kingdom Connection Point

You have the same peace available to you by the Holy Spirit that Jesus had while living on the earth. Therefore, when you step into your stance to hit a shot, connect into this peace that the Lord has for you. You really can feel this rest in your heart. The beauty of this is the benefit of rest you will feel in your body. Your muscles will relax, which will be a great benefit to your golf swing. All the great athletes play their best when their muscles are relaxed and their minds are at ease. Some call it "the zone." I call it communion. Again, it only takes a split second to make this connection with the Lord. Receive His peace, look at your target and hit your shot. I think you'll find the results to be much better.

Chapter 3
Alignment from the Place of Victory

The classic definition of sin is "to miss the mark." When you hear the word *sin*, you typically think of what you're doing wrong. There are times to honestly evaluate your life before the Lord. If you're missing the mark, He's faithful to help you overcome in a loving way. However, I do not like to focus on the negative aspects of life. When you examine the list of things to "meditate upon," in **Philippians 4: 8**, you don't find Paul encouraging us to place our focus on negative ideals. Rather, he wants us to meditate upon whatever is true, noble, just, pure, lovely, of good report, virtuous and praiseworthy. What you behold is what you become. I'll choose victory over defeat any day.

Recently, in prayer, I sensed the Lord whispering into the ear of His Church the words, "It is finished." It struck me as a reminder for God's children to live from the place *of* victory, not *towards* victory. This is true because of Jesus' finished work on the cross. If the Victorious One lives inside of you, than you are victorious. If you're a born-again believer and think that you're still a sinner and not a saint, than you have it backwards. Paul starts out his letters to the different churches in the New Testament, addressing them as "the saints." He did not address them as sinners. Why? Because the new nature of a Christian is not that of a sinner. The new nature is that of a saint. You may still sin on occasion, but that is not your nature. If you think you're merely a sinner saved by grace, than you have still missed the mark. You're marked as a saint, who lives in relationship with the Most High God. This is hitting the mark. This mindset should be your focus. It makes all the difference in the world. Start each day from the place of victory you have in Christ. This is the alignment with God that Jesus paid for.

Speaking of alignment, this is a crucial part of hitting good golf shots. The way you align your body and club at the start of every shot can make a huge difference in the outcome. Golf has been described as a game of inches. This is very true. Therefore, it is very important to have your club face aligned properly towards your desired target. Being misaligned by only a few degrees can result in missing your target by several yards. Missing the target by several yards can cause your golf ball to land in some spots you definitely don't want it to be in. So, let me help you get aligned correctly.

Getting Set to Overcome

It all starts with seeing the target line clearly. Because you hit the golf ball standing to the side of it, it's hard to accurately see the target line. It's much easier to see it when you're standing behind the ball, looking directly at your target. So, this is where we'll start.

I like to start two to three paces straight behind the ball on the desired target line. My eyes start on the target and then work their way back on a straight line to the ball. I visualize the shot I plan on executing. I then fix my eyes on *something* that is just in front of the ball and on the desired target line. The object is typically six to twelve inches in front of the ball. This could be a leaf, a patch of dirt or a discolored piece of grass. Whatever my eye sees, that is what I become fixated upon. The key is to find something that is on the target line which you can clearly see. The number one goal from here is to align my club face so that it is aimed directly at this object. For the purpose of this teaching, I will call it a leaf. I'm now intent on putting my club down behind the ball so that it points directly at the leaf. If my club is pointing at the leaf, it will be pointing at my desired target.

I then walk to the left of the golf ball and approach it from an angle that is perpendicular to the target line. It's much easier to see the target line when coming at it from 90 degrees. I step in with my right foot first, leaving my left foot slightly behind my right. When I step in with the right foot, I plant it at a 90-degree angle to the target line. Next, I place the club head behind the golf ball, with my eyes still focused on the leaf. I'm intent on making sure the club face is pointing directly at the leaf. You can see what this looks like in the picture on the previous page. This assures me that I have my club face pointing at the target, which is call a *square* club face. If it is pointing to the right of the target, it's called *open*. If it's pointing to the left, it's called *closed*. In golf, it's *hip to be square*. Sorry, bad joke!

It's time to bring my left foot into position. While I'm standing to the left side of the golf ball, I want my feet, knees, hips and shoulders to be parallel to the target line. Therefore, I imagine a line that is parallel to the target line right in front of where my feet rest in the setup position. This is called the *toe line*. I bring my left foot forward, so that my toes are flush against this parallel line. Finally, I spread my feet to the right and left along the toe line. When practicing this approach, it's helpful to lay alignment sticks or golf clubs on the ground, parallel to each other. One will be on your target line and the other on your toe line. I've demonstrated this for you in the following picture.

Aligned from the place of Victory

I'm now ready to follow the procedure discussed in Chapter 2, to complete the setup position. Of course, I maintain the alignment of my club face at the leaf, in order to stay square to the target line. I'm now ready to execute a solid golf shot. When you get used to this procedure, it's easy to repeat. You'll notice that the professional golfers on both the PGA and LPGA Tours go through this very alignment process almost every time they hit a shot. It's of the utmost importance. It's hard to consistently hit the ball at your desired target if you're not aiming at it. So, take an extra 10 seconds before you hit your shots and go through this alignment procedure. Proper alignment, partnered with a solid grip and stance, is a necessary step to victory in golf.

Kingdom Connection Point

Know that you're already victorious as you go through the process of aligning your shots. Approach your shots from the place of victory, not hoping that you will be victorious. As a believer, you have been properly aligned with God in the position of an overcomer. Because He has already won the victory, you have already won. This is who you are as one of His beloved saints. When you stand over the ball, look at your target through this lens of victory. You will find that this positions you to hit some great shots and live your life as an overcomer.

Chapter 4
The Building Blocks of Body Rotation

The foundation is meant to be built upon in order to achieve the ultimate structure you've set out to build. The grip and setup have been established, so let's build upon them with the rotational motion of your body. More specifically, the way in which you rotate your hips and shoulders in your backswing and downswing. Amongst many great instructors in the world, there is a debate as to the dominant motion that serves as the foundation of the golf swing. This debate is between how the body rotates and the way the arms swing the club. Simply stated, body rotation vs. arm swing. While I understand both sides, I personally have landed on establishing the body rotation first and partnering the arm swing in later. I believe that establishing the body rotation as the foundation of the golf swing serves the majority of golfers better. Therefore, let's get started.

I want you to establish your setup exactly as prescribed in the Chapter 2. However, I'm going to take the arms out of the equation at this point. I want you to accomplish this by crossing your arms in an X across your chest. The picture below helps demonstrate this for you. (See image on facing page.) With your arms removed from contributing to any part of the *golf motion*, you're forced to call upon the rotational motion of your hips and shoulders. At times, I will refer to your hips as your lower body, the shoulders as your upper body.

As you start the rotational motion of the backswing, I want you to feel your hips and shoulders rotating around your spine. Many refer to this as a central axis rotation. In the process, you'll feel weight shifting to your right leg. This is due to the fact that your left shoulder and knee will be moving further to the right from their starting position. I'll give more specific details on this later. Your shoulders will rotate more than your hips. Typically, your hips will rotate 45 degrees and your shoulders 90 degrees from their starting positions.

The extra degrees of rotation of the shoulders upon the hips creates resistance or torque. This is very necessary in creating a core source of power in the swing. Some of you may remember the old toy airplanes, where you wound up the propeller that was attached to a rubber band. By winding up the rubber band tight, you created the centrifugal force necessary to spin the propeller and cause the plane to take off. In the same light, think of the resistance you're creating between the rotational motions of the upper and lower body. You're creating the centrifugal force necessary to send the golf ball into flight with power.

In the midst of this rotational motion, it's also very important for you to maintain the proper height and body angles. You may recall that you established a setup height when taking your stance over the ball. You should also remember that you created a spine angle and knee angle, when setting up to hit a shot. You need to maintain these angles (and height) as you rotate your body in the backswing. When you rotate your hips and shoulders the full 45 and 90 degrees, you'll have completed an adequate amount of turning within a full backswing.

If you change the angles and height that you started with as you make your backswing rotational motion, you'll then have to make compensations for them as you make your downswing. Compensations create room for errors, which in turn require more adjustments with your body and the club in order to produce a solid strike of the golf ball at impact. This isn't easy. In fact, it's very difficult. While a few of the PGA Touring professionals are exceptions to this, it's not the norm. I also understand that your angles will change some as you make the descending blow into impact. I'll address this point in a moment and in a later chapter. Regardless, as you make your rotational motion in your backswing, please work hard to maintain your initial height and angles throughout. It will work to your advantage.

At the top of the backswing, notice that your left shoulder will have rotated to the inside of your right thigh. Your knees started at the address position approximately 12 inches apart. As you rotate your hips to the top of your backswing, you want to maintain this distance. You do not want to separate the knees from each other in the rotational motion. I'll get more specific on these points in Chapter 5, but I want you to have a general understanding of these points as you begin to build your body pivot.

OK. What do we do with all the torque that has been built up through the backswing rotational motion? You release it. It's time to start the downswing rotational motion. Keep in mind that your arms are still across your chest in the form of an X. Don't worry, I'll be adding the action of the hands and arms soon enough. Remember, at this point, I'm establishing the foundational motion of the body pivot.

As you unwind your hips and shoulders, you'll feel them turning towards your left side. Specifically, you'll feel your weight transferring from your right leg to your left leg. This weight transfer is in conjunction with your left hip moving laterally towards your target as it rotates. It's also because your right shoulder, hip and knee are now in the process of rotating to the left side of the golf ball's position on the ground. You may feel a spinning motion as you go through this process of unwinding your body.

What happens to your height, spine angle and knee angle as you're making this motion? Good question. You may feel a slight, descending angle as you rotate your body. In particular, this will be through the impact zone, where you would feel the hit of the golf ball with the club. I know your arms are still folded across your chest, but you can sense this. As you analyze touring professional's golf swings, many have a greater flex in the knees as they deliver the club into impact. Many also have a lower head position at impact than their height at address. However, for the purpose of this drill, I still want you to feel like you're maintaining the same height and angles you established in the backswing through this impact zone. I want you to focus on continuing to rotate the hips and shoulders to create a fluid feeling in the motion.

Now, let's complete your body rotation all the way to your finish position. As you continue to rotate to the top of your follow through, you'll need to release your body from its setup height and angles. If you don't, you'll shut down your follow-through. This will produce a decrease in speed and power in your swing. You definitely do not want that.

You'll release your weight off the back foot, which allows your hips to fully turn to your left side. You'll want to come up onto the toes of your right foot. This will allow your playing partners to see the entire, bottom side of your right shoe. You'll finish at your full height, balancing very tall on your left foot. Your left leg needs to be straight in order to balance your body weight on the left side. This is called *posting*, and I will address it in more detail later in the book. As you can see in this picture, the middle of your waist will be pointing at your target. Your shoulders will turn approximately 45 degrees to the left of your target.

This full shoulder turn to the top of your follow through will be the result of some amazing momentum created by the body rotation. When we connect the action of your arms and the club into this motion, you'll be amazed at the power that can be generated while hitting a shot. This rotational motion is like the engine of a car. When it synchronizes with your arms and club, you can *push the pedal* to produce some amazing speed. Speed is good in the game of golf. Establish a solid, rotational motion in your upper and lower body, and you'll start to generate more speed. This will translate to more power. I like power!

So, work on this drill, and you'll be on your way to having a great body turn in your swing:

1. Establish your setup position with your arms across your chest in an X.
2. Rotate your hips and shoulders to the right around your spine, about 45 degrees with your hips and 90 degrees with your shoulders.
3. Maintain your setup height, spine angle and knee angle as you rotate back.
4. Unwind your hips and shoulder back to your left side.
5. Again, maintain your height and angles as you turn through the impact zone.
6. Release out of your hitting height and angles as you rotate to your finish position.
7. Your hips will point at your target, and your shoulders about 45 degrees to the left of target.
8. You will be on the toes of your back foot, balanced in a tall finish position on your left foot.

Earlier in this chapter, I used the word *core* to help define the body rotation as a main source of power in your golf swing. Core is a very valuable word in golf and life. You can also think of the word *core* in terms of your values, guiding principles, defining declarations and much more. You need to develop these ideas out for your own life. You need to have a core and live from it. For the purposes of this book, I'm defining core as the Cross, resurrection and indwelling of Jesus Christ.

Chapter 5
The Core of Golf and Life

The Cross and Resurrection! Books upon books have been written upon these subjects. A multitude of sermons have been preached throughout the centuries, giving deep insights into the wonders of these events. They're not to be limited to the religious ceremonies conducted across the world on Good Friday and Resurrection Sunday. Because they're *core*, they're intended to have daily focus and implications. You need to study them closely and implement them in your way of life. I'm not going to go into a deep, theological study on these events. However, let's take a closer look and connect some simple ideas on relating to this core in your golf swing.

The Cross! Some theologians believe the Cross is the central point of time for all of history, whether before or after the event. After the fall of man in the Garden of Eden, man and woman proved they couldn't live a life without sin. They couldn't keep the Ten Commandments. They certainly couldn't fulfill all the laws established by the Sadducees and Pharisees. Sin was winning. Humanity was losing. Separation from God's true intentions was the result. Continually sacrificing animals was proving to be religious ceremony, resulting in little-to-no transformation. You could call it dead religion. Because of the separation, a blood sacrifice was required to overcome the sin. Atonement was still necessary in God's plan. Here comes the heart of the Father!

The Father's heart said something like this, "I sure love these children that I created. I'm heartbroken that their sinful way is creating a separation in our relationship. I really want to be close to them always. The animal sacrifices are not drawing their hearts closer to

Mine. There is a better Way. There is a Way that will result in the life of communion that I've always desired. That Way is through the blood of My son, Jesus! Because My heart longs for them, I'm ready to implement the atonement that will satisfy my requirement for all of eternity. Jesus, it's time to set them free from the judgment that came through Adam's choice. It's time to extend the free gift of life. It's Your time." **(See Romans 5: 17-21)**

So, Jesus was born in Bethlehem to a virgin girl named Mary. . He lived a perfect life with no sin, in order to become sin for us. I love **2 Corinthians 5:21** that states, "For God made Him who knew no sin to be sin for us, that we might become the righteousness of God in Him." He demonstrated the *love* and *power* of God in ways that were mindboggling to those around Him. His teachings astonished the wisest of the day. His miracles raised the bar as to what *normal* should look like. Simply put, He revealed the Father, His ways and His kingdom. Through it all, He didn't break the law, yet took the full punishment of it on our behalf. The full punishment meant death on the Cross. A death that was more painful and brutal than most any human will ever know. Yet through this intense torture, the Scripture shares that, "for the joy set before Him, [He] endured the cross." **(See Hebrews 12: 2c)**

Joy? Endured? Seriously? I don't know about you, but I doubt I would be experiencing joy while someone was driving iron stakes through my hands and feet. I don't think I'd be *pressing on* when my body was experiencing pain I'd never thought possible. In the context of this passage, the word *joy* relates to that of calm delight and great gladness. The word *endured* relates to the idea of persevering, bearing and abiding. Why would Jesus bear upon Himself this much pain with gladness and delight in His heart? I believe the answer is simple. He had joy in knowing He was fulfilling the Father's will. He was delighted in knowing that He was making *a new and living way* that would bridge the gap of separation forever. In the heart of Jesus, you were worth it. You always have been and always will be! The Cross was Heaven's Hallmark Card with the clear message of "I love you." If you're still trying to overcome sin through your own efforts, you need to stop. The blood of Jesus will always be enough to atone for your sins. So, let this be true and stop striving out of your own abilities. His finished work is more than sufficient. If you haven't already, work out your salvation, today, based upon the Cross, His love and His gift of eternal life through Jesus Christ. It's the most important issue you will ever have to come to terms with in this life. Your salvation was made possible on the Cross of Calvary.

The Resurrection and Indwelling Life! Following His death on the Cross, Jesus descended into Hades and completed some unfinished business. He took back the keys that were stolen by the devil when he deceived Adam and Eve and, today, gladly gives the keys of the Kingdom to us. **Revelation 1:18** declares, "I am He who lives, and was dead, and behold, I am alive forevermore. Amen. And I have the keys of Hades and of Death." **Matt. 16:19** states, "And I will give you the keys of the kingdom of heaven, and whatever you bind on earth will be bound in heaven, and whatever you loose on earth will be loosed in heaven." This accomplishment is of immense significance to every child of God and deserves your personal study time to gain deeper understanding. It gives insight into who Jesus really is as the Champion of Heaven. The Victorious One! It should also excite you to consider what you can accomplish with the *keys of the kingdom of heaven*. The possibilities are amazing.

Where would we be without the Resurrection? We'd be lost, perishing and the most pitiable of persons on the planet. **(See I Corinthians 15:12-19)** Verse 17 makes it plain by stating, "And if Christ is not risen, your faith is futile; you are still in your sins!" But Christ is risen! His resurrection is what allows a believer to be made alive. **Verse 22** states, *"For as in Adam all die, even so in Christ all shall be made alive."* If you are a believer, than you are in Christ. If you are in Christ, you have been made alive by Him.

It was necessary for His resurrection to occur before the indwelling and baptism of the Holy Spirit could be achieved. His resurrection life has always been intended to be your resurrection life in God. Take a close look at **Romans 6:4, 11**. The phrases, *"so we also even"* and *"likewise you also,"* have a very simple and direct meaning. His resurrection life is for you! This is why John wrote the words, "as He is, so are we in this world," in **1 John 4:17c.** He wasn't referring to the Jesus on the Cross. No, he was referring to resurrected Jesus at the right hand of the Father. He was referring to the fully victorious, conquering, overcoming, fully glorified Jesus. This is the Jesus that lives inside of you. This is the Jesus that you're to display to the world around you. His resurrection life is that which you are to reveal. Living from your position in the resurrected Jesus is a life of His love and power in all areas. This is the life He paid for. Jesus didn't die on the Cross and resurrect to the right hand of the Father for you live defeated, ridiculed by fear and trying to survive. Rather, He did it to enable you to live as He did and even greater. You'll either believe the truth of **John 14:12** or you won't. "Most assuredly, I say to you, he who believes in Me, the works that I do he will do also; and greater works than these he will do, because I go to My Father." When Jesus said, "Because I go to My Father," He was referring to the resurrection. I choose to believe His words and thoughts towards me over the lies of the enemy. I believe this resurrection life is for every day. Come and live this way with me! It is the best version of you, after all.

OK, Chuck. I believe in the Kingdom truths you just shared. You have me excited to live this *resurrection life* every day. But how do I incorporate this into my golf swing? Good question. Recall with me that I'm referring to the Cross and Resurrection as the core of life. They are eternal and the effects of these events never stop. They're continual.

I've already described the *core* of the golf swing as the rotational motion of the body. The upper and lower body need to *wind up* on the established body angles in the backswing, and *unwind* with rotational movement, all the way through the impact zone to a complete finish. In order to keep the motor of your golf swing running, the body rotation must continue to move. Like the Cross and Resurrection, the rotational motion of the body is continual. The following Kingdom

Connection Point will help bring the implementation of this into clearer focus.

Kingdom Connection Point

When you're hitting a golf shot, take a moment to meditate upon Jesus' fulfillment of the Father's will, by His completed work on the Cross. Marvel at what He accomplished for you through the Resurrection. Visualize these Heavenly conquests in your mind and tap into them as you feel your body rotating throughout your swing. My hope is that you'll experience true, resurrection life in your spirit as you rotate your body throughout your swing. Why not? The resurrected King is in you at all times. Therefore, enjoy Him at all times.

Chapter 6
The Core: A Closer Look

I hope you enjoyed the last chapter on the Cross, Resurrection and rotational motion of the body. They are such important components in achieving a successful life and golf swing. At this time, I want to go a little deeper into some specifics. These specifics will focus on the shoulders and hips, the movement of the knees, rotation around the spine and lateral rotational motion throughout the swing. This chapter will get into more *hard core* golf mechanics and theories.

Let's start with the backswing and look at the shoulder rotation first. When rotating your shoulders in the backswing, you'll want to achieve approximately 90 degrees of rotation, as described previously. However, it's important that your left shoulder travel on a *level line* when rotating to the top of your backswing. When you're at your address position, visualize a line between your left and right shoulders. As you rotate your shoulders, let your left shoulder rotate upon this line as you complete your backswing. You'll find that your left shoulder will end up almost where your right shoulder began. If you drop a line straight down from the middle of your left shoulder, it will intersect the inner portion of your right thigh. Please keep in mind that the shoulder rotates in conjunction with maintaining your spine angle. When you maintain spine angle, your shoulders will rotate on a *level plane*. This is a simple fact related to God's anatomical design of your body.

Here's a simple drill to help you establish this. Place a club across your chest. You'll hold it in place by crossing your arms in the X position described in Chapter 4. Observe the line formed by the club across your chest. As you rotate your shoulders in the backswing, let your left shoulder travel across the line formed by the club. After doing this drill a few times, try it with your eyes closed. It's good to *feel the motion* in the drill, in order to translate it into your actual golf swing. This drill is also handy to determine whether or not you're rotating your shoulders a full 90 degrees. Compare the shaft across your chest with that of your target line. You'll see if you've achieved a *full 90* or not. Study the following pictures to gain more understanding of these points.

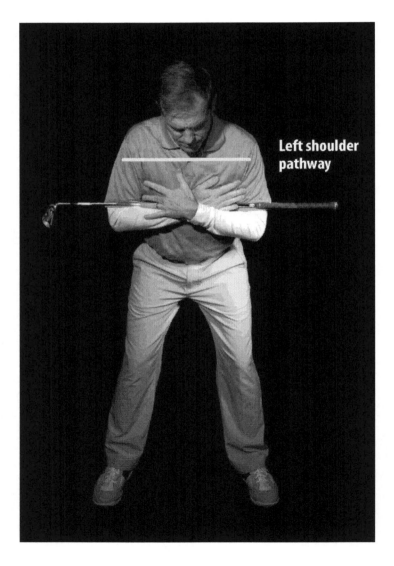

Left shoulder pathway

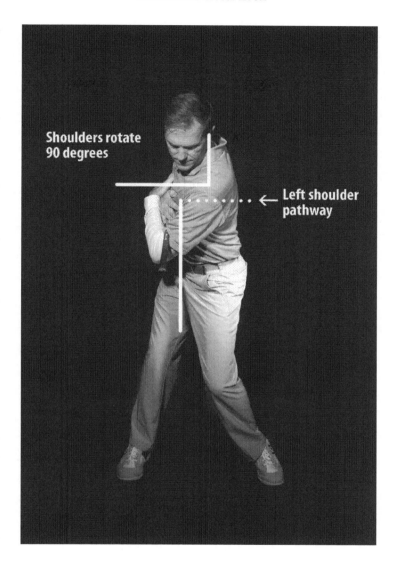

As a word of caution, I want to point out some things to stay away from when rotating your shoulders in the backswing. Make sure that you do *not* rotate your shoulders well past 90 degrees. Over rotating your shoulders can easily cause your upper body to tilt back towards your left side. Within the tilting motion, your spine angle will lean back to the left. This is commonly referred to as a reverse pivot. Over rotation also allows the shaft to travel much farther than necessary at the top of the backswing. It's wasted motion. Both issues cause a variety of challenges on the downswing, which are hard to overcome. Suffice it to say, rotating your shoulders 90 degrees is plenty.

If you let your left shoulder drop down, which will keep it from rotating towards your right side, your spine angle and head will be lowered. Your weight distribution will also shift to your left side. This is another source of the dreaded reverse pivot. A reverse pivot in the backswing will require compensation in the downswing. This compensation is usually lifting your head and spine back up, and shifting your weight back to the right side through impact. Many golfers with this issue end up with their weight on their right foot at their finish, or worse. Perhaps you've seen someone hit a golf ball and fall backwards, away from the target as they complete their swing? That is a classic sign of someone with a reverse pivot. I've given many lessons where I place my hand on the student's left shoulder and force it to rotate on this *level line* all the way to the top of their backswing. Many of them have related that it feels like the shoulder is moving *way to the right* of what they're used to. It may feel weird, but I've often said to "trust the weirdness." Also, please remember that it's in the context of a rotational motion, not a sway to the right.

Conversely, you don't want to let your left shoulder raise up in the midst of the backswing rotation. If you do, you'll be lifting up your head and spine. This alters the angles you'll establish in your setup position and will cause many problems. If you lift up in your backswing, you'll have to drop back down in your downswing to try and make contact with the ball. Easier said than done! This is what I call "Up and Down Golf," and it doesn't work very well at all. This swing approach creates very little torque due to the lack of body rotation. It also produces many *fat* shots, due to the club crashing down into the ground behind the ball. This golfer looks like they're chopping down upon the ball, rather than swinging through it. This isn't a good approach and you'll want to stay away from it.

So, use the drill to your advantage in creating a beautiful shoulder rotation in your backswing. You may even want to do this drill in a mirror or have a friend watch you, in order to get valuable feedback. Also, be sure to go after the correct shoulder rotation with a club in your hands. You hit the ball with a club in your hands, so be sure to emulate the feeling in this manner as well.

Hebrews 13:8 states, "Jesus Christ is the same yesterday, today and forever." This passage is in the context of the church, remembering the teachings brought to them by the leaders over them. They didn't want them to be influenced by all the other doctrines swirling about them at that time. The point is to stay true to the teachings about Jesus, because Jesus is unchanging. Jesus is perfect and will never have a need to change. He's been, and always will be true to Himself, as His own self. We'll spend all of eternity discovering the vastness of His perfection. It doesn't matter what century or season of history you were born into; He will always remain the same. This is why you can always trust the Lord and walk in peace with Him. You can only trust that which you know will remain constant. Jesus is truly that!

From this passage in **Hebrews 13:8**, I want the next golf thought to focus on the word *same*. Remember that the way your hips and shoulders rotate in the backswing will have everything to do with keeping your spine and knee angles the same. It makes sense that if these angles are not changing, than your shoulder will rotate in a level manner around a fixed point. If you change the angles of your head, spine and legs, your shoulders are going to change with them. It's just the way God made you! Therefore, keep the angles the same as you rotate the body in the backswing. You can trust a pivot that's built upon constant angles. You'll get much better results from positions you can trust.

Kingdom Connection Point

Build the shoulder rotation in your backswing upon the fact that Jesus is unchanging and always remains the same. Meditate upon the constancy of His entire being and hold onto this image as you achieve a level rotation in your shoulders. This is a big key for me in my own golf swing, as I have a tendency to slightly lift my spine angle as I rotate to the top. I'm motivated by this verse, in order to achieve the goal of keeping my angles the same in the backswing. I enjoy the challenge as I connect with the person of Jesus. You can do the same.

Let's now take a closer look at the way your hips rotate in the backswing. As mentioned previously, you want to achieve approximately 45 degrees worth of hip rotation. To reiterate, this amount of hip rotation will create a solid base upon which the shoulders will rotate the prescribed 90 degrees. As the 45 degrees of hip rotation are resisting the 90 degrees of shoulder rotation, you'll be creating a significant amount of torque. Remember, this is a great source of power in your swing. In order to achieve this, I want you to understand that your hips are rotating and not swaying to the right. I've had many students through the years say, "I have to load up my right side in my backswing." While I understand what they mean by that phrase, it has some major *fine lines* to it. When they'd use the word *load*, I knew they meant the desire to create rotational torque. Unfortunately, many of these students swayed to the right with little rotation of their hips in their effort to *load* their right side. As a result, they certainly weren't creating torque that would result in more power. They were actually achieving quite the opposite.

There is a classic golf tip that says, "Feel like your hips are turning inside a barrel." It remains a solid idea today. When you rotate your hips properly around a fixed point, the outside of your right hip will actually move backwards and to the left of its original position. Take a look at these pictures to gain further understanding of this point. In the first picture, notice the line that's been drawn from the ground to the outside of the right hip. In the second picture, with the hip rotation complete, notice the gap in space between the line and the position of the right hip. Please note that I'm not asking you to shift your hips over to your left side. Rather, I'm wanting you to see how the hip functions within a central axis rotation. You can do this yourself by sticking a shaft in the ground, causing it to rest against the outside of your hip. When you rotate your hips, you'll find the right hip moves away from the shaft and does not press into it.

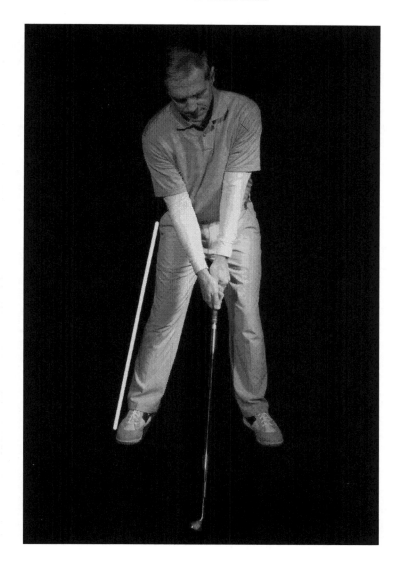

Another way is to have a buddy hold a shaft against the side of your hip at address. When you make the proper hip rotation, you'll see the same result. You'll create a gap between the shaft and your hip. Again, I don't want you to merely shift your hips to the left. I want you to clearly understand that I'm teaching you how to rotate your hips around a central point. It may feel a little weird but remember to "trust the weirdness."

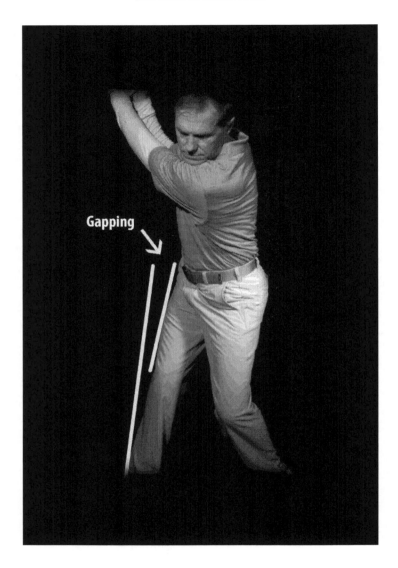

Gapping

What about the action of the knees in the backswing rotation? This is actually a very important question that doesn't receive a lot of attention in most instructional circles. The reason it's important is because the action of the knees is directly related to the movement of the feet in the golf swing. There have been some great players through the years, like Johnny Miller, who made the movement of their feet and knees a top priority. Brandt Snedeker once told me this was of great importance to his mechanical approach to the golf swing. As these, and many other great players demonstrate, your left foot may come off the ground and onto the toe, as you rotate your hips in the backswing. While many modern-day instructors teach to keep the left foot flat on the ground, I don't mind it coming up off the ground. This can actually aid the rotation of the hips and produce fluidity in the overall backswing motion.

As I've already stated, it's important to maintain the knee angles established at address in your setup position. While it doesn't have to be exact, it'll certainly feel that way. In the backswing rotational motion, I want you to focus on keeping the distance between your knees constant. By keeping the angles and distance between the knees the same, it greatly aids in maintaining balance and a synchronicity between the two legs. It's like they're working together as a team. A good drill you can do to help maintain the distance between your knees is to put a ball between them. A small beach ball is a good one to use, as it's light and gives some flexibility. As you make your rotational motion in your backswing, keep the ball between your knees with a slight pressure. If the gap between your knees widens, the ball with drop. After practicing the drill with the ball, take some swings without it. You should be able to emulate the feeling you had with the ball, as you maintain the knee angles.

Here's an example of what you don't want to do. If you let your right leg totally straighten as you make your backswing, your left knee will increase its flex to compensate. The gap between your knees will widen significantly. Thus, the ball will drop to the ground. Your right knee will be moving too far away from the target line as the right leg locks out. It'll then be forced to thrust forward towards the target line, as you attempt to hit the ball. This typically causes the lower body to *fall back* toward the right side as the hips rotate. This has a negative effect on swing plane and body angles, causing problems that are undesired. More on this later in the book.

Kingdom Connection Point

I don't want to give you another Kingdom principle to utilize, in respect to the finer points of the hip rotation and knee action in the backswing. You can easily apply the thoughts that've already been established. The Cross, Resurrection and Constancy of who Jesus is, are more than sufficient to apply to these ideas. Rather, I want you to start exploring the Scriptures for your own ideas. Pray to God and trust that the Holy Spirit will show you how to utilize for these points. While I want you to apply my teachings, I truly want you to develop your own approaches, based upon what the Lord is speaking to you.

Not sure you can hear God? Be encouraged with the words of Jesus in **John 10:27.** *"My sheep hear My voice, and I know them, and they follow Me." If He's your shepherd, than you're one of His sheep. If you're one of His sheep, than you can hear His voice. If anyone's told you otherwise, I'll submit to you that they're contradicting Scripture. He may not speak to you in audible English. He may speak to you with thoughts, pictures, dreams, feelings, etc. That's for you to figure out as you pursue your relationship with Him. Just make sure that what you're hearing doesn't contradict Scripture, as God would not speak those types of things to you. Regardless, know that your Lord is speaking to you, and you can hear. Go ahead and try it now. In a stance of fellowship before Him, pray and have fun listening. You may be surprised to discover that He's been speaking to you for many years—only in a way you never knew was Him.*

Well done. You've worked through many points in constructing the core rotational movement of the backswing. However, I want to finish this off by looking at one more item. . It's the debate between I central axis rotation and utilizing the lateral rotation in the backswing. Do you rotate around a fixed, spine angle; or do you allow the spine to move a bit to the right as you rotate to the top? Some wonder if you should keep your head totally still in the backswing, or if you should allow it to move to the right? These are good questions, as this is a very important issue to understand.

So, here we go. This is my official statement on this debate. I prefer to maintain a central axis of rotation around your spine, but allow flexibility for some lateral motion of the spine within the turning motion. One student will adapt well to a central axis rotation approach, while another needs to create a little more space *behind the ball'* with some movement to the right. It all comes down to utilizing the approach that gets the best results for the student.

Let's compare these two approaches. The first approach has the shoulders rotating around the spine in a central position. Thus the phrase, *central axis rotation.* A lot of torque has been created by the resistance between the upper and lower body. It's a very solid position. The second approach utilizes the same amount of shoulder rotation, with movement of the spine to the right in the process. At the most, I would say the movement is about three to four inches to the right of the initial spine angle. I certainly do not want you moving more than that.

Here's the fine line between the two. When you add extra movement to the right, you're inserting a *potential for error* in the swing. However, if the movement is minimal, I believe you can control it and still produce quality golf shots. Also, if you're going to move the spine to the right, please make sure that it's within the context of a rotational motion. As mentioned earlier in the book, do *not* sway to the right. The reason some players need the extra three to four inches to the right is to create some *extra space* behind the golf ball. This space can make it easier to release the clubface at impact, avoiding the fade or slice to the right of your target. If you're going to rotate a bit to the right of center, know that you'll need to make up that distance to left in your downswing.

Be careful not to create too much space by moving your spine too far to the right. You can actually produce a scenario where the clubface, due to this extra space, releases too easily through impact. This will result in a hook to the left. It's good to video your swing. This will allow you to draw the appropriate lines to accurately analyze how much your spine is really moving. At the end of the day, while I prefer the central axis rotation, you should choose the approach that's best for you!

Choice. What a beautiful word. It reveals the loving nature of our Father. A love that doesn't control or dominate you. The heart of a Father that honors you to the extent that He allows you to make choices that are against His will. He'll let you make choices that aren't good for you. Why? He so deeply values you that He will not force relationship with Him upon you. He's purely authentic, and His nature will only allow Him to produce that which is also authentic. He's proven, to the point of death, that He wants this type of communion with you. He's made the Way possible. He desperately wants you to know this love that pursues you. Yet, He puts the choice in your hands.

You can simplify your choices into one of two camps: life or death. Another way of saying it is that our choices can be rooted in the life that comes from God's Kingdom or the decaying death that comes from the enemy's kingdom. Light vs. darkness. Good vs. evil. Life vs. death.

After 40 years of leading the Israelites in the wilderness, Moses spoke a commandment before them, in order to restore the nation of Israel back to God. In **Deuteronomy 30: 19-20** the passage reads, "I call heaven and earth as witnesses today against you, that I have set before you life and death, blessing and cursing; therefore choose life, that both you and your descendants may live; that you may love the Lord your God, that you may obey His voice, and that you may cling to Him, for He is your life and the length of your days; and that you may dwell in the land which the Lord swore to your fathers, to Abraham, Isaac, and Jacob, to give them." This commandment was also made near the end of Moses' life, which was of great importance. People's last words are usually ones to closely heed. Yet, the choice still belonged to the Israelites.

Kingdom Connection Point

This thought is intended more for your life than the golf game. From a golf perspective, know that you can choose between a central axis rotation and one with lateral motion. As you make your choice, be thankful that you serve a God who doesn't control you! Be thankful for God's love and the freedom He bestows upon you. In life, we all make many choices every day. Most of them have small consequences, while others are large. Regardless, all of them have an effect on us and others. All of them are rooted in life or death, blessings or curses. None of them need to be taken lightly. Choose life over death today and enjoy the wonderful consequences associated with life. Which one will you choose?

Chapter 7
The Downswing Rotation

Let's now begin the transition to the downswing, rotational motion. You've coiled your upper and lower body in such a way that you've generated a significant amount of torque and power. However, the torque and power need to be released. It's time to use what you've stored up. It's time to unwind the body rotation throughout the downswing motion.

Please, remember that your arms are still in the shape of an X across your chest. The action of the arms, hands and club are coming soon. As you start to unwind the hips, legs and shoulders, I'm hoping the motion in your downswing, will be a natural one. However, let's get specific.

A question that's been asked for decades is, "what part of the body starts the downswing?" Is it the legs, hips, shoulders, hands, etc...? When you slow the golf swing down with high powered video equipment, you see that the lower body starts first. There have been studies done, which reveal certain core muscles are the first to fire as the downswing is started. Some professional golfers will actually start to unwind their lower body before the upper body has completed the rotational motion in the backswing. This is due to the need for the lower body to achieve a weight transfer to the left side of your body to support a solid impact position. I'll explain this in more detail when I teach on the impact zone.

Let's examine the lower body first. As your hips rotate back to your left side, you'll feel weight transferring to your left leg. We actually have a drill at the academy called the "bump drill." In this drill, we place a shaft in the ground just to the outside of the student's left foot. The shaft extends upward to the outer edge of their left hip. From the top of their backswing, we have them *bump* the shaft with their left hip. This requires them to activate their lower body and transfer some weight to their left side. If you have a stick of some kind, you can stick in the ground and give it a shot.

Your left foot, if you let it come off the ground in the backswing, will plant itself down on the ground again. The hips will continue turning towards your left side, allowing your right hip to *come around* until your belt buckle is pointing at your target. If your hips are pointing to the right of your target, you'll know that you've not turned them enough. I played some of my best competitive golf, by spinning my hips as the first move I made from the top. The only thought in my head was, *turn!* While you don't want your lower body to turn too fast ahead of the upper body rotation, the feel of turning your hips from the top is usually a productive one.

The angles of the knees and leg action are of critical importance in the downswing rotation. Remember to maintain the knee angle established in your setup position, all the way to the top of your backswing. We talked about keeping your *hitting height.* As you start to unwind your lower body in the downswing, your knee angles will actually change a little bit. They'll start to increase in a downward motion. Another way of saying it is to flex your knees a bit more as you start the downswing. Here's why. If you've ever tried to hit a golf ball, it doesn't take long to figure out that you must hit down for the ball to go up. You often see the touring professionals take large divots out of the grass as they strike their irons. The grass divot will go flying down the fairway. This is the result of a descending blow of the club head into the ball.

Therefore, as you turn your hips in the downswing motion, you'll feel a slight increase in the flex of the knees as you approach the impact position. Some golfers have to be more intentional with this *flexing down* of the knees, as they tend to straighten their legs too quickly in the downswing. These golfers stand up early and typically hit the top of the golf ball. This results in the ball rolling on the ground and not flying in the air. We used to call this shot the dreaded *worm burner*.

Your right knee will be traveling towards your left side and pointing towards the golf ball as you come into the hitting area. In conjunction with this, your right foot will roll to the left, with your weight shifting to the inside of the foot. This helps to maintain the distance between the knees as you rotate the hips.

Right knee angles towards the ball. Right foot rolls toward instep.

If you let your right knee move straight out towards the target line, you'll be inhibiting the weight transfer and hip rotation to your left side. You'll also increase the distance between your knees and allow your weight to stay back towards your right foot. Your hitting motion is towards your left side, so let your right knee point in that direction as you rotate through impact.

As you continue this motion past impact to your finish position, your left leg and knee will straighten up. The momentum of the swing, and a large percentage of your body weight, will be moving to your left side. Therefore, it's important to have a solid left leg upon which to collect this momentum and weight. Many teachers call this *posting your left leg*. If you don't post your left leg and keep it bent to your finish position, you'll have a hard time balancing. You'll most likely lose your balance to the right and be forced to step in that direction, as not to fall over. So, don't hesitate to let your left leg straighten up as you rotate to your finish position. In conjunction with this, many great players feel their left hip traveling behind them, away from the target line, as they complete the rotational motion. This is all in the context of producing a *full finish*.

Your right knee will continue to move forward, towards the left knee, as you rotate your hips and finish the downswing…Eventually, your right leg will straighten out as well, as you complete the rotation of the hips and legs. In order to achieve this, you'll want to let the bottom of your right foot come off the ground, balancing on your right toe. If you keep your right foot down, you'll shut down the rotation of the hips into a full, finish position. This will cut off the rotational force you created in the backswing and needed to unleash in the downswing. Ultimately, you'll lose distance in your shots. I'm sure you don't want that. My childhood teacher, Phil Darbyshire, used to tell me, "let your right knee kiss your left knee at the finish." This is still pretty good advice today. Whenever you'd say goodbye to Phil, he'd always leave you with a smile and his token phrase, "down the middle." Phil was a good man and helped shape my golf game in my early years.

Let's now examine the rotational motion of the upper body in the downswing. The lower body leads, but the upper body must follow in order to achieve good golf shots. Please recall that your shoulders rotated around your spine in the backswing. This will remain true in the downswing. As you transfer your weight to the left, your spine will remain *angled back* as you come into the impact zone. Your left shoulder will be higher than your right. The fact that your right hand is lower on the club than your left is another reason your left shoulder will be lower than your right through the hitting area.

While the right shoulder is clearly lower than the left in this zone, I still want it to continue rotating. Many great teachers communicate the idea of *covering the ball* with your right shoulder as you turn through impact. This phrase relates to the right shoulder rotating on a more level approach, as opposed to dropping very low into the hitting area. I will expand on this problem in a moment.

We're now coming into the hitting area. As you approach impact, your shoulders will already be pointing slightly left of your target line, and your right shoulder will be rotating forward towards the golf ball. The spine angle is of crucial importance as the upper body unwinds in the downswing. Remember, that I prefer a central axis rotation, as prescribed in the backswing. This is still true in the downswing. While the rotational motion of the downswing is to your left side, you need to maintain some *tilt* in your spine to the right in the process. While your lower body will be transferring weight to your left side, you'll need to allow your spine to angle backwards towards your right side at approximately a 25-degree angle. This can feel a little awkward but is quite necessary to achieve quality golf shots. The picture on the following page brings clarity to this point.

If you allow your spine to move too far to the left, you'll most likely be swaying and not rotating. You've probably heard somebody say, "I got ahead of that one," after hitting a poor shot. This phrase refers to losing the tilt of your spine angle too far to your left side as you swing through impact. You haven't maintained a central axis of rotation. This shuts down the motor and power available to your swing. If you allow for some lateral spine movement to the right, in the midst of your backswing, you'll have to allow your spine to move back to the left as you rotate into impact. Here is the fine line. If you moved

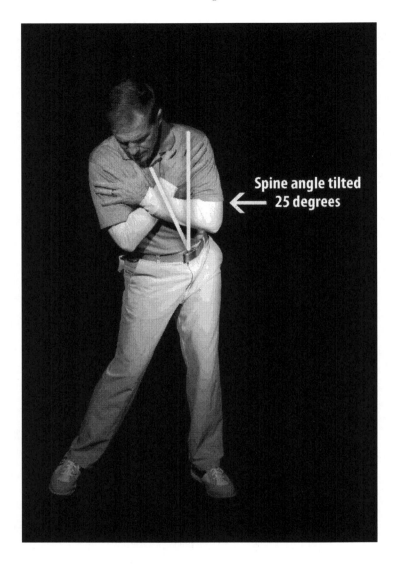

three inches to the right in the backswing, you won't want to move more than three inches to the left as you come into the hitting area. While there is *room for error* in this type of move, it can be done successfully at a high level. Ben Crenshaw was one of the greatest players of his era and won more than one major championship with this move. Regardless, please remember that this occurs as your shoulders continue to rotate.

As you rotate the shoulders past the impact zone, you'll begin to release your spine angle upwards to your finish position. You'll regain your full height as you come to rest in a balanced position on your left leg. You want to keep the shoulders rotating all the way through. As a result, your chest will point approximately 45 degrees left of your target.

A big problem I often see when working with amateur golfers, is that their right shoulder drops down too far as they begin the downswing. They drop the right shoulder, which in turn makes the left shoulder rise very high as they approach impact. This creates a very steep shoulder angle. (See image on previous page.) Their sternum points very high towards the sky, and their upper body hangs back a long time. I describe this as their right side staying too far *underneath*. With the left shoulder too high and the right shoulder too low, the centrifugal force we're wanting to generate through impact tends to go away.

Try the following drill to overcome a steep shoulder angle as you swing through the ball. Hit shots with the ball well above your feet. You can do this on the side of a tee box. The contour of the tee box will force you to swing your shoulders on a more rounded plane. If you drop your right shoulder, you'll probably stick the club in the ground behind the ball. You can also make practice swings, imagining the golf ball is at the height of your waist. You should easily feel how your right shoulder stays higher (and covers) as you swing through, as opposed to dropping down low. Once you *feel* this move in the practice swing, work on emulating it when hitting the ball off the ground. You can do it!

Some players generate enough club head speed with the power of their arm swing to overcome a steep shoulder angle at impact. However, it's a rarity amongst the common golfer, and many *other things* have to be correct to pull it off. A flowing, rotational motion of the shoulders will certainly serve you better as you play golf.

At the start of this chapter, I stated that the torque and power generated within your backswing need to be released. It's now time to use what you've stored up. If you don't do something with that which you possess, what's the point? Do you ever feel that way with respect to your Christian life? Do you ever feel like you know more *about* Jesus' words than knowing what to do *with* His words? Knowing vs. Doing. It's a necessary examination. I'm not saying you shouldn't gain more wisdom. **Proverbs 4:7** declares, "Wisdom is the principal thing;

therefore get wisdom." It's good to know more, as long as you don't let knowledge puff itself up into a state of arrogance. It's good to know more about Jesus and His ways, as long as you apply it to your life and to those around you. There's a big difference between knowing *about* Christ and really knowing Christ. Being able to give a Theological lecture on His image is not the same as being transformed into it.

Christianity is not merely about sitting in meetings and having someone talk to you about Jesus. It's a life of faith and action that comes from communing with Him and applying His commandments. . **I John 3:24a** states, "Now he who keeps His commandments abides in Him, and He in him." If you guard His words in your heart so that you don't lose sight of them, you'll be compelled to do what He says. **I John 5:3a** declares, "For this is the love of God, that we keep His commandments." The commandments of Christ require action in order to keep them. Notice that keeping His commandments is rooted in the love of God. Therefore, I'm not trying to put a *works* trip on you. Rather, I'm wanting to motivate you to take action because of love. Let love lead; for love requires action.

Let me explain it this way. Jesus asked Peter three times if he loved Him in **John 21: 15-17**. Peter answered emphatically "YES" all three times. Each time Peter answered, Jesus responded with "feed My sheep." Jesus wasn't trying to make Peter perform and work for His love. He was showing Peter that true love for Him places such a value on His words that action is a natural outcome. It's not that we *have* to feed His sheep. We *get* to feed His sheep. It's an honor to take action for Jesus out of a heart of love for Him, in order to keep His commandments.

If Christians don't take action and follow the commandments of our King, how then will the fallen world around us know that we are followers of Jesus? **Acts 11:26c** declares, "And the disciples were first called Christians in Antioch." Keep in mind that this declaration was made years after the ascension of Christ. Antioch was a very wealthy and powerful city. Yet it was also a wicked city. Followers of Jesus showed up in the city and started preaching the Lord Jesus. Many in

Antioch became believers, and the church grew. Interestingly, the word *called*, in this passage, has a unique meaning. While it definitely carries the meaning of a title bestowed upon someone, it also relates the idea of one that constitutes a business. A citizen of Antioch, after observing those who were following Jesus, would be convinced that they were truly about the business of Jesus. They made Jesus' heavenly agenda their personal business on the earth. Thus, they were called Christians due to the way they resembled Jesus. Obviously, the people of Antioch were observing the Christians' actions. These people took what they received from Jesus and did something with it. You can do the same. You have just as much authority and power as those that shifted the culture in Antioch. Let your knowing turn into doing. He's worth it!

Kingdom Connection Point

When you start the downswing rotational motion, think upon what Jesus has empowered you with, and how He intends you to impact your surroundings with it. Take what you have received and do something with it. Envision the fullness of what this life with Him can look like. Now transition these thoughts into releasing the torque and power that you've stored up on the backswing. Let it go without passivity. Let the rotational motion flow through, all the way to your finish position. Don't waste it through minimal action. Let it be full so that your life and golf game will be fulfilling!

Great work. You've completed the rotational motion of the upper and lower body throughout the backswing and downswing. You've a tremendous foundation in the body pivot, upon which, we can now build the rest of the golf swing. As we move forward, I'm going to be teaching you how to use your arms and hands to swing the club. I'll be going deep into swing plane, shaft angles, forearm and wrist angles, and many other details. However, please remember that all these teachings will be synchronized with the rotational motion of the body. They must work together in harmony and proper timing. Let's get after it!

Chapter 8
The Holy Trinity, Swing Plane
& the Takeaway

It's finally time to implement the use of your arms and hands. You don't have to keep your arms in an X across your chest any longer. You can let them fall down naturally. Take your grip and establish that beautiful setup position we established at the beginning of the book. Speaking of the setup, I want to point something out to you. Notice the triangle that is formed between your two elbows and hands when you set up to hit a golf ball. As we learn how to hit a golf ball the working relationship between these three components of the triangle is very important.

Moving forward I'll refer to this triangle as the *trinity triangle*. Father, Son and Holy Spirit. Oh, what an amazing mystery wrapped up in the greatness of the true, living God. While I'm not going to try and theologically unwrap the Trinity, I will be connecting you to your relationship with the Father, Son and Holy Spirit. This will be achieved at different positions throughout the golf swing. (See photo on the next page.)

The left elbow will represent God the Father sitting upon His throne. (**See Revelation 7:10**) The right elbow represents Jesus, who sits at the right hand of the Father in the heavenly realm. **Ephesians 1:20** presents this beautifully as it relates to the power the Father worked in Christ, "when He raised Him from the dead and seated Him at His right hand in the heavenly places." The hands represent the Holy Spirit, our great Helper. "But the Helper, the Holy Spirit, whom the Father will send in My name, He will teach you all things, and bring to your remembrance all things that I said to you." **John 14:26**

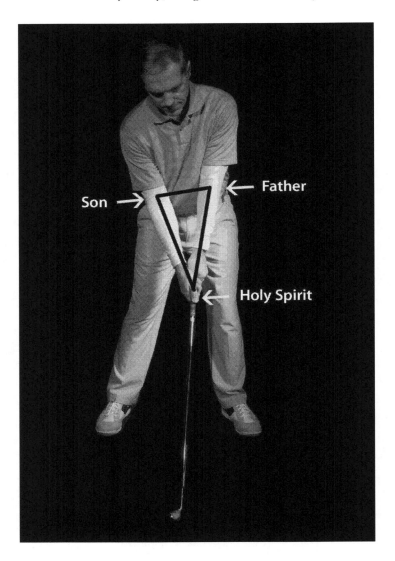

I believe the Father, Son and Holy Spirit are always ready to reveal more of Themselves to us, in every area of life. As we now begin to closely examine the path of the club in the backswing and downswing, stay ready to relate to the Trinity in many unique ways. The Lord may speak to you in a way in which you didn't expect. I love it when He does that! Let's get started.

Swing Plane! This is a phrase that's been used in the golf instruction world for many years now. With advancements in technology and video analysis, swing plane is a regular part of the instructional vernacular. With these advancements, have come many debates over swing plane and the best way to swing the club. So, what exactly is swing plane? A plane is a flat surface upon which an object can travel. In our case, that object is the golf club. The club is comprised of the grip, shaft and club head. However, it's important to know how the club relates to that of the swing plane.

When you achieve the proper setup position, clubs are designed to fit your body in a specific way. This is why working with a professional club fitter can be very important when buying set up clubs. The club head rests on the ground on the target line. The shaft is angled upward towards your body, so that it will point into your waist at your *belt buckle*. If you were to extrapolate the shaft through your body, it would come out your lower back and extend behind you. When utilizing video analysis, I'm constantly drawing a line along the shaft and up, through the body. Many instructors simply call this the plane line. (See image on previous page.)

Please note that the angle established by the golf club will vary with each club. Your pitching wedge, which is a shorter club, rests on a steeper or more vertical angle. The driver, which is your longest club, has a much flatter shaft angle. The varying lengths of clubs, degrees of loft and shaft angles, are necessary. This is what allows us to hit the ball longer or shorter, depending upon what is required for the shot at hand.

Back to swing plane. If you were to lay a flat surface upon the club in your hands, extending to the right and left sides of the shaft, you'd create a plane. In order to visualize this in your mind, imagine a piece of plywood resting upon your club at the address position. You now have a flat surface upon which your club can travel. The following picture will help you understand and better see what I'm referring to. (See image on next page.)

Now that we've established a working definition for swing plane, let's get started with the first movement in the backswing. This is referred to as the *takeaway*. As you begin the backswing, I want to see your hands, the club shaft and club head traveling along the face of the plane. This is what I refer to as being *on plane*. For the sake of further definitions, if you swing your club to the right side of the plane line, I call this *outside the plane*. If you swing the club to the left side of the plane line, I call this *inside the plane*. I'll make reference to this as we continue, so lock this away in your mind.

Why is being on plane important? It's due to the fact that the swing plane originates on the ground at the target line. The target line points down the fairway towards the flag or desired landing spot. This is where we want the ball to go. Therefore, it makes a lot of sense that we want our club to swing upon the plane that relates directly to our desired target. I hope the Holy Spirit just dropped some Kingdom thoughts into your heart after reading this last sentence. I'll expound on this at the end of this section. Back to the takeaway. In the first foot of your backswing, I want to see the club traveling along the face of the plane. The trinity triangle has remained constant without changing the angels of the triangle. Some teachers refer to this as a *one piece* take-a-way. I like to think of it as the unity between Father, Son and Holy Spirit. Let's keep going.

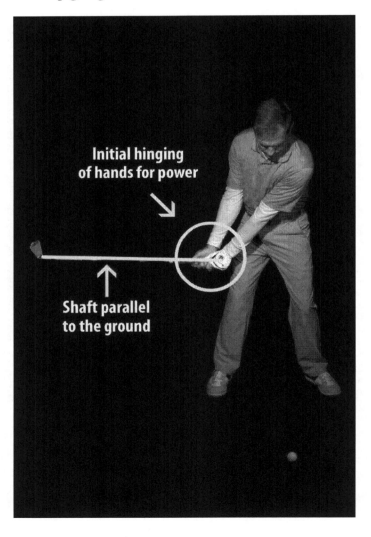

Initial hinging
of hands for power

Shaft parallel
to the ground

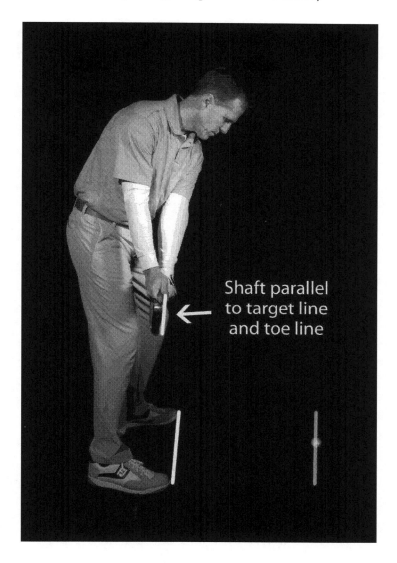

Shaft parallel to target line and toe line

As the club continues to swing in the backswing, I want to see the hands and shaft continue on the face of the swing plane. Your hands have swung just outside of your right thigh, and the club is rising higher. The shaft is approximately knee height at this point. However, notice that the trinity is starting to change the angles of the triangle. The *Holy Spirit* (your hands) is starting to hinge the shaft upward a little bit. Because of this hinging motion, the shaft will achieve a position that is parallel to the ground, while still remaining on plane. This is the beginning of creating some power in the swing. We definitely want power! Also notice that *Jesus* (your right elbow) is starting to fold a slight bit. The *Father* (your left elbow) continues to remain straight and solid. The previous pictures will help you see this position more clearly.

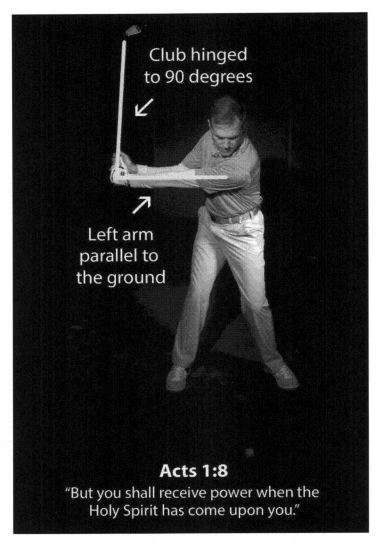

As we move into the next stages of the backswing, the hands and club will start to go higher. As this occurs, the hands, shaft and club head will leave the original plane. Watch and see what happens. The club will swing higher, with the hands coming up to the height of your sternum. Through this stage, the *Trinity* is actively at work. The *Holy Spirit* has hinged the club to a 90-degree angle between your left arm and the shaft. I call this *setting the angle* with many of my students. You'll feel this in the hinging motion of your wrists, as your left arm stays straight. The left arm will be parallel to the ground at this stage of the backswing. You don't want to let the *Father* (left elbow) fold and break down, in order to achieve a more vertical shaft angle. Let the *Father* stay constant as the *Holy Spirit* (wrists) does the hinging work for you.

By keeping the left arm and elbow straight, you'll be creating necessary width in your backswing. This width is the distance from your chest to your hands. Take a close look at the picture below to thoroughly inspect the angles of this position.

Because of this hinging, the shaft is now on a more vertical angle through your right shoulder, not your waist. I call this *plane number two*, which is a steeper plane. This is why I don't believe in a one plane swing. If you extend a line through the shaft, pointing down towards the ground, the line will hit between your target line and feet. Some teachers prefer to see this line intersect the target line, which is fine. I like to see it intersect a few inches inside the target line, with a slightly steeper shaft angle. With respect to your hands, I want them to intersect your chest in between your sternum and right bicep. You can clearly see the shaft angle and hand position I'm referring to in the picture on the following page.

The more vertical shaft angle is because of the way that the *Holy Spirit* (wrists) has hinged the club. This is necessary to achieve power in the swing. If you don't want any power, then don't hinge your wrists. Try it for yourself. Swing the club back and through, keeping your wrists as stiff as possible. You'll notice quickly that it doesn't generate much speed. Now swing it back and through, utilizing wrist hinge. You'll notice the whipping sound that is generated by the speed in the club head. This speed relates to power. I want power in your golf

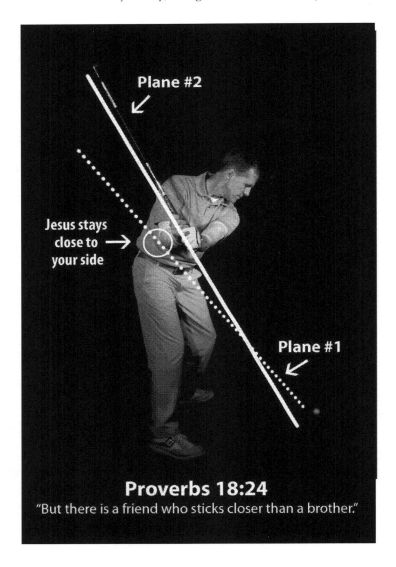

swing, and I assure you that the Holy Spirit is into empowering your life.

Jesus was very intent on His disciples receiving power in their lives before He ascended into Heaven. **Acts 1:8** declares, "But you shall receive power when the Holy Spirit has come upon you; and you shall be witnesses to Me in Jerusalem, and in all Judea and Samaria, and to the end of the earth." These are the last words Jesus spoke before ascending to heaven. Last words are very important, which is why He commanded them to stay in Jerusalem and to wait for this great Promise. Jesus knew that His disciples needed supernatural power before being released into ministering the truth of the Kingdom.

The power Jesus is referencing here was manifested on the Day of Pentecost, as shown in Acts 2:1-4. This is when the Holy Spirit came upon the disciples in the upper room. **Verses 3-4** say, "Then there appeared to them divided tongues, as of fire, and one sat upon each of them. And they were all filled with the Holy Spirit and began to speak with other tongues as the Spirit gave them utterance." This is commonly referred to as the Baptism of the Holy Spirit. While I believe that a Christian has the Holy Spirit within them upon believing and being water baptized, the Baptism of the Holy Spirit is a different event in the believer's life. This is when the Holy Spirit comes upon you and gives you more of His power. **(See Acts 8:12-17)** Many Samaritan men and women had believed in Jesus and were water baptized. If these believers had received all of the Holy Spirit that could ever be made available to them, through belief and water baptism, then why did Phillip pray for them to receive the Holy Spirit? **Verse 16** states it clearly. "Or as yet He had fallen upon none of them. They had only been baptized in the name of the Lord Jesus." They had believed and been baptized, but the Holy Spirit had not fallen upon them. When the Holy Spirit comes upon you, He gives you the power Jesus referred to in **Acts 1:8**. This word *power* comes from the Greek word *dunamis*, which means "miracle working power." Give yourself permission to receive this miraculous power that Jesus paid the price for. It's spectacular.

It doesn't make you better than another believer in the eyes of God. It doesn't make you more loved by God. It's simply receiving more of God's power because of His great love for you. I can honestly say that this event radically changed my life upon receiving it in January of 1995. If you're not sure you've been baptized in the Holy Spirit, then I assure you that you want it. It's incredible, and the Holy Spirit's gifts are truly amazing. Hunger for more of what the Holy Spirit has for you and then ask God for it. **Luke 11:13** asks, "How much more will your heavenly Father give the Holy Spirit to those who ask Him." Ask! He's a good Father who gives good gifts. God's *more* is really good!

Kingdom Connection Point

When using your hands to hinge the club midway through your backswing, connect to the power of the Holy Spirit made available to you through the words of Jesus in **Acts 1:8**. *While the hinging motion taps into the natural power obtained through the laws of physics, know that you are spiritually powerful as a child of the King. Know that the Holy Spirit has more power for those that eagerly desire His gifts. Ask for more and enjoy your connection with the living God.*

At this stage in your backswing, I want to bring your attention to another factor. Notice that your right elbow has folded to approximately a 45-degree angle. This folding motion is happening in conjunction with the hinging of the club by your hands. In the picture captured from the face-on angle, you'll see that the right elbow extends slightly below the left arm, which remains straight. If the right elbow is at the same height as the left arm, that's fine. The point is that the right elbow needs to be folding at a downward angle at this point. You don't want to have your right elbow pointing up where you can see daylight in between it and your left arm. This separation, or what some have referred to as a *flying right elbow*, can cause some significant problems.

If you feel you have this problem, a good way to overcome it is to place a small ball (like a beach ball) in between your elbows at address. Your goal is to keep the ball between your elbows as you make your backswing, all the way to the top. To achieve this, you'll have to allow your right elbow to fold and maintain its distance from the left elbow, as established at address. Many touring pros use a training aid called the Tour Striker Smart Ball. You can also place a glove under your right armpit. To keep the glove tucked under your armpit, you'll have to keep the right elbow pointing down and close to your side. Both of these approaches truly work and could be a great help to you.

Within the trinity triangle, the right elbow represents Jesus. So, what is *Jesus* doing at this stage in your backswing? He's staying very close to your side. I love **Proverbs 18:24** which declares, "A man who has friends must himself be friendly, but there is a friend who sticks closer than a brother." Jesus is that friend who sticks closer to you than you can imagine. He even calls you His friend in **John 15:15.**

Jesus also declares in **Matt. 28:20**, "I am with you always, even to the end of the age."

The Hebrew perspective on the word *close* is that of clinging to or joining together. Jesus is that friend who clings to you and will never leave or forsake you. The New Testament reality for the Christian is that which is found in **Col. 1:27.** This reality is "Christ in you the hope of glory." I would say that Christ taking up residence inside of you is Him truly joining together with you. Now that is close!

Kingdom Connection Point

As your arms are swinging the club through the middle section of your backswing, acknowledge the closeness of your Savior as your right elbow folds by your side. Look at every area of your life and know that He's right there in the midst of it all. Look for Him in your circumstances, whether good or bad, and surrender to His ways. You don't have to go searching for Him, as He is already there with you. Listen to His loving voice and receive His embrace.

Chapter 9
Going to the Top

It's time to finish the backswing. The arms have swung the club about two thirds of the way back, bringing your hands to the height of your sternum. Your left arm is parallel to the ground. The shaft has been hinged to a 90-degree angle, with the club on a more vertical plane. The shaft is now passing through your right shoulder. The *Holy Trinity* has been at work in the midst of it all. Now, let's go higher and get to the top of the backswing.

How do you complete this backswing all the way to the top? This is an important question. You need your hands, arms and club to go higher so that your backswing is not too short. Some people lift their hands and arms up to a steeper position. Some break their elbows upward, in order to get the club to a higher place in completing their backswing. Unfortunately, these efforts cause more problems that are hard to fix.

The key is to allow the entire unit of the arms, elbows, hands and golf club to turn to the top with the rotation of the hips and shoulders. The word *unit* is a good one for you to relate to at this point in the backswing. I'm defining this unit as the trinity triangle and golf club combined. Together they are one unit. The trinity triangle formed the beautiful angles previously described. Now let the entire unit be carried to the top by your rotational motion. Don't add extra, unnecessary work to the elbows and hands. Please recall that we're building the pathway of the club (swing plane) upon the rotational motion of the hips and shoulders. The rotational motion is correlated with the Cross and Resurrection of Jesus. Speaking of Jesus, notice how He (your right elbow) is still angled down and close to your side. He's just never going to leave or forsake you. This is the foundation we're building the rest of the house upon. If you need help keeping *Jesus* close to your side at the top of your backswing, remember the drill of keeping a glove tucked under your right armpit. Keeping Him close will always be beneficial to your life and swing. As you turn the unit to the top, I want you to feel your left arm stretching across your chest. As you do this, your left arm will form approximately a 45-degree angle, relative to the ground. In the picture from the front, you can see that your hands should be slightly higher than your head. They'll also be out to the right of your head, keeping the *width* in the backswing that I prefer.

Full hinge

Gapping of hip

High Place *of* **Humility**

Maintain distance between the knees

James 4:10
"Humble yourselves in the sight of the Lord and He will lift you up."

In looking at the picture below from the side, notice the amount of space between your hands and head. This is what I call *depth*. This depth is accomplished by stretching your left arm across your chest, and not letting your left arm break down at the elbow. When this depth is achieved, it sets you up to achieve a better downswing plane when delivering the club through the impact zone.

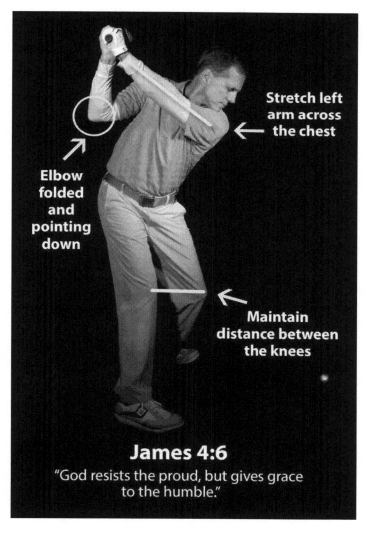

Stretch left arm across the chest

Elbow folded and pointing down

Maintain distance between the knees

James 4:6

"God resists the proud, but gives grace to the humble."

Of course, this is what determines the direction your golf ball with fly—either towards or away from your target. I cannot reiterate this enough; the stretching of the left arm across your chest achieves the width and depth I want you to gain at the top of the backswing. Both these factors will make it easier for you to produce a better *angel of attack* on the downswing. A good drill to do, to achieve the width and depth desired at the top of the backswing, is one called *touch the wall*. I learned this from an outstanding teacher, partner and friend, Ben Pellicani. You can see how this drill works in the following two pictures.

In the drill, you take your setup position against a wall. Your rear end will slightly make contact with the wall. With your hands together, as if you were gripping a club, make a backswing by turning your hips and shoulders. As you do so, make your hands touch the wall behind you. You'll have to stretch your arms out wide and behind you to actually touch the wall. You'll feel some muscles you haven't used in a while,

I'm sure. In achieving this position, you'll be creating the width and depth I'm looking for. Repeat this a few times to allow your brain to assimilate this motion. Finally, put a club in your hands and reproduce the *touch the wall feeling* at the top of your backswing. If you can, try it with a mirror out to your side, so you can see how your left arm stretches across your chest and produces the depth we've been discussing.

I'm focusing on the action of the arms, hands and swing plane in this section of the book. However, I want to point out an important component of your hip turn. Earlier in the book I mentioned the *gapping* of the right hip as you rotate to the top of your backswing. In the *touch the wall* drill, you can also work on this gapping. When you set up against the wall, you can draw a line on the outer edge of your right hip. Perhaps some electrical tape will work for you if you don't have another means. When you rotate your body and touch the wall with your hands, you'll want your right hip to separate away from the line. The gap is back towards your left side and indicates the desired, central axis rotation discussed.

If you look back at the picture taken from the side, you'll notice the shaft is resting at the top of the backswing in a parallel relationship to the target line.

This is a great position at the top. It also makes sense geometrically, as it maintains a relationship between the shaft and the target line. Your golf ball sits upon this line, and it points to your desired target. If the club in your hand is pointing well to the left or right of this parallel position, you'll then have to make a compensation on the way down to overcome the flaw. If you don't change the angles established by the trinity triangle and club when you properly set the angle earlier in the backswing, the shaft should easily find the parallel relationship at the top. Give it a shot. Again, a mirror would be a great help to you when examining these positions.

Going Higher! That's really what we just achieved by going to the top of the backswing. How do you go higher in the ways of God? There are many different perspectives on what this looks like. Some like to pray for hours to access the Heavenly realm and move the heart of God. Some like to preach the Word. Some like to soak in worship and invite His presence into their lives. Others prefer to minister to lost souls, bringing the great news of salvation through Jesus' death and resurrection. Personally, I like and enjoy all of it. All of it taps into the higher ways of the Kingdom.

For the purposes of this teaching, I want to focus on the *higher place of humility*. **James 4:10** states, "Humble yourselves in the sight of the Lord, and He will lift you up." The context of this chapter in James is dealing with the problems of life that come from selfish lusts, misdirected pleasures and friendship with the world. James is urging believers to submit to God, draw near to Him and resist the ways of the devil. This is the posture of the heart he's pressing into when he wrote of the wisdom of humbling yourself in the sight of the Lord.

What does it mean to humble yourself? The word *humble* means "depression," "to depress" or "to be made low." Are you saying that God wants me to be depressed? Yes and no. No, in the traditional sense of what it means to be depressed. The typical perspective on depression is that of an emotional state or way of feeling. This type of depression is very real for some people and I feel for them. So, no, God doesn't want you to live in this type of depression. He made the way of freedom from it, so you don't have to.

What I'm saying is that it's good for you to be depressed from a Kingdom perspective. The Scripture says to humble yourselves. This requires action. This is an intentionality of the heart. You have to do it, as nobody else can do it for you. It's a choice to depress yourself or to make yourself low. The beauty of this choice is that it's done *in the sight of the Lord*. This can be translated as "in the presence of." It's a glorious stance in life to walk humbly with the Lord in order to make Him high. It's to resist the selfish ways of man. It is drawing closer to God.

As you do so, **James 4:10** teaches us that God will then lift you up. Where will He lift you up to? It's to a place of high regard or a position of greater power. This is what humility accomplishes in your life. It unlocks the door to high regard and power. Don't forget that "God resists the proud, but gives grace to the humble," as stated in **James 4:6**. Making yourself low allows God to take you up higher. Such is the way in God's Kingdom. It's the opposite of how man typically thinks. Man's way doesn't consider humbling himself, in order to gain a position of power. Man's way is to make others lower than yourself in order to climb the ladder of success and power, usually at the expense of other. Jesus didn't take this approach. Jesus humbled Himself by coming to earth in the form of a man. Out of this humility, He was obedient all the way to death on the cross. **(See Phil. 2:8)** The beauty of His humility to the point of death is that it allows you to be humble to the point of new life. This way of humility truly is higher. It's better. It's honorable and true. Make the point to humble yourself and watch Him lift you up.

Kingdom Connection Point

As you turn the trinity triangle and golf club to the top of your backswing, do so with a heart of humility. Reflect upon the humility Jesus portrayed during His life here on earth. Make it a moment of worship as you make yourself low in His presence. You really can do this, as you practice the drills I taught you. Enjoy this moment with the Lord as you take the high place of humility.

Chapter 10
The Downswing Attack

I *hate* the devil! I hate the way he operated out of pride to try and rival God. I hate how he tried to overthrow His Kingdom. I hate the way he deceived Adam and Eve in the Garden of Eden, altering the current state of humanity on this earth. I hate the way he uses fear and lies to attack God's children. I hate the way he walks about like a roaring lion, seeking whom he may devour. (Please note that he is not truly a lion, and he can only devour those who give him permission. He is defeated forever and has no authority compared to King Jesus!)

Why am I focusing on the devil at the start of this chapter? The reason is that I want you to visualize the golf ball as the head of the devil. I want you to unleash a mighty blow upon his head. As you strike down and through the impact zone, I want you to crush him. It's going to take some power to accomplish this. It'll require the proper shaft angles and positions within the trinity triangle. It'll take an increase in speed. But you can do it. Let's get to it.

Please recall that you will now be unwinding the hips and shoulders in the rotational motion taught earlier in the book. This body pivot is still the foundation upon which the action of the arms and club is supported. If the body rotation collapses, everything else falls apart. Remember the *bump drill* I taught you in Chapter 7? This helps you establish some weight transfer into your left side as you begin the downswing. This weight transfer helps to support the rotational motion all the way to your finish.

I now want to focus on the first movement of the trinity triangle and club from the top of the backswing. Follow me on this, as this is a very important point. Halfway through the backswing, the *Holy Spirit* (your hands) hinged the club to a steeper shaft angle. As you turned the entire unit to the top of the backswing, this unit essentially traveled up the face of this steeper plane. However, remember that the golf ball is resting on the flatter plane that was established by the club at the address position. This flatter plane also originates at the target line, which is the direction you want the ball to fly. Therefore, you must shallow the shaft on the way down in order to regain the original, flatter plane that the golf ball lies upon. Simply put, you're on a steeper plane at the top of the backswing and you must achieve a flatter plane on the angle of attack into the ball.

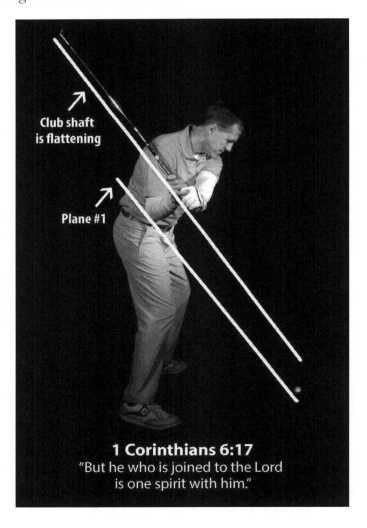

1 Corinthians 6:17
"But he who is joined to the Lord
is one spirit with him."

So, how do we do this? I'm going to approach it from a few different angles, focusing on the action of the *Holy Spirit* (hands) and *Jesus* (right elbow) as you start the downswing. I want to see your hands moving down in a direction towards the original plane. You can even visualize them moving in a line towards the golf ball. The hands will pass through the right shoulder on the way down, maintaining some depth behind your head. (See image on the previous page.)

This is crucial. If you allow your hands to travel in front of your body on the way down, the club will descend too steep and have a hard time regaining the original, flatter plane. Therefore, I want you to feel as if the *Holy Spirit* doubles the effect of gravity on the hands, so they will travel downward and not out in front of you.

Jesus is starting to get more aggressive at this point. Notice how the right elbow has increased its fold and is tucking in even closer to your right side. You can see in the picture below how the right elbow is clearly visible below the left forearm. (See picture on the next page.) This is a result of the increased *folding and tucking* motion of the elbow. This is just like our beautiful Lord. He refuses to leave your side and abandon you. The *Father* (left arm and elbow) is ever constant, staying straight and solid. I love how the *Father* stays solid, which keeps the trinity triangle intact. This allows *Jesus* and the *Holy Spirit* to hinge and fold accordingly. If the left arm and elbow were to break down in your swing with a severe bending motion, the right elbow and wrists would not be able to function the ways in which I've been teaching you. The shaft and club face angles, necessary to hit good golf shots, would not be achieved. I love how all three Members work together in harmony, supporting each other in order to achieve the same goal.

The Trinity does this in your life as well. The Father, Son and Holy Spirit will minister to you in different ways, while working together to help you advance in the ways of the Kingdom. The Father may enlighten you while reading His Word. Jesus might share a picture with you during your prayer time. The Holy Spirit can bring a thought or feeling to you, in order to move you off one path and onto another. The bottom line is this: stay open to how the Trinity can relate to you as you go through your days. You might be surprised how frequent and simple it really is. It's also wonderful and what you were made for!

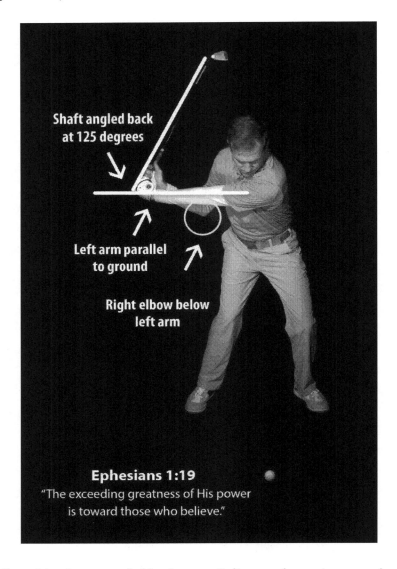

Power! At the start of this chapter, I discussed wanting to unleash a mighty blow of power upon the head of Satan. Take a look at the angle between the shaft and left arm at this stage in the downswing. Notice how the shaft angle has increased dramatically. At this point in the backswing, I wanted you to establish a 90-degree angle. However, at this point in the downswing the angle has increased to approximately 125 degrees. This greater lag in the shaft angle is setting you up to unleash the club head with significant speed and power through the hitting zone.

This increased shaft angle is achieved by your hands and right elbow working together in this first move of the downswing. As the hands are pulling the handle of the club down, there needs to be an increase in the *cocking action* of the wrists towards your right shoulder. The right elbow increases its fold towards your right side, which aids the cocking action of the wrists. As these two motions are achieved harmoniously, they affect the shaft by angling it backwards. This also aids the shaft descending on the flatter angle we discussed earlier in this chapter. This is so important for you to understand and implement into your swing. In looking at the photo from the front, notice how the shaft is angled back over your right shoulder and head. This increased shaft angle is what a lot of teachers refer to as *lag*. Lag is good. It's your friend. Lag helps to produce speed and power.

In this first move from the top of the backswing, decreasing the angle between the shaft and left arm is not good. In fact, it's really destructive to a golf swing. This is commonly referred to as a *casting motion*. When casting a fishing rod, you release the angle of the rod above your head. This is great for fishing and bad for golf. When you cast the club in the golf swing, you're releasing the angle of the wrists too early. This throws the shaft away from your right side. Typically, the angle between the shaft and left arm decreases below 90 degrees. This casting motion is equivalent to throwing your power right in the trash can. It ultimately throws off the proper sequence and timing of delivering the club into the golf ball at impact. It creates a multitude of problems through the hitting zone and into your finish position. Outside of an improper grip, the casting motion is the most devastating move for most golfers. So, go fishing in the pond or for the souls of men, but not in your golf swing.

A good way to check your shaft angle on the way down is to

observe your positions in front of a mirror. Stop the club when your hands reach the height of your sternum and see where the shaft is angled. If it's angled back towards your right shoulder and head, you're doing well. If the shaft is pointing to the right of perpendicular, and less than 90 degrees, then you're casting.

In this position, I want your right elbow to be visible below your left arm. When your right elbow increases its fold, it's a crucial part of helping the shaft flatten in the first move down from the top. If your right elbow is hidden behind your left arm, then it hasn't folded enough. This type of *right elbow issue* also makes it hard to flatten your shaft angle on the way down. It'll do the exact opposite and make the shaft come down too steep. As you already know, this isn't what you want. If the mirror reveals a casting motion, then increase the folding of your right elbow and hinge the shaft backwards with your wrists. Look for the changed positions in the mirror. Do it slowly and hold the angles in your new positions for a few seconds. This gives your brain time to form new neuromuscular pathways that'll hopefully become repeatable.

Let's get back to the issue of power, but let's look at it from a Kingdom perspective. **Ephesians 1: 19-20** declares, "And what is the exceeding greatness of His power toward us who believe, according to the working of His mighty power which He worked in Christ when He raised Him from the dead and seated Him at His right hand in the heavenly places." This passage comes from one of Paul's famous apostolic prayers. These truths are connected to his words in **verse 18** when he says, "That you may know." Paul's prayer reveals that he wants believers to be aware of and understand what they have in Christ. So, let's take a closer look at what you have, and who you are as a believer.

Paul wants you to know of "the exceeding greatness of His power" that is towards the believer in Christ. God's power by itself is more than exciting. This is the same Greek word *dunamis* that we examined before. This is miraculous power. However, Paul makes his point with greater emphasis by adding the phrase, "the exceeding greatness of His power." The word *exceeding* relates the idea of a javelin thrower, throwing way beyond his normal mark. It would easily be a new, personal best. The word *greatness* simply means "to magnify." Therefore, the message that Paul is trying to instill in our hearts is of significant importance. It's for us to understand that the miracle working power God has given to us is much larger and far beyond what we've experienced up to this point in our lives.

To further his point, he continues with the phrase "according to." I love phrases like this in the Bible, for they're pregnant with deeper meaning. He's setting us up for the context in which he's referring to. The context is God working His dominion over death when He raised Jesus from the grave and seated Him at His right hand. When you became a believer in Christ, you were automatically qualified to receive this magnitude of power. Power to raise the dead. That is why Jesus says in **Matthew 10:8** to, "Heal the sick, cleanse the lepers, raise the dead, cast out demons. Freely you have received, freely give." Jesus has given His believers this type of power, and He wants us to exercise it as evidence of His kingdom being at hand.

Here's the big question: have you given yourself permission to be this powerful? Have you decided that "the exceeding greatness of His power" is just as much for you today as it was for the disciples in the first century church? These are important questions that you need to answer. I'm telling you that the answer to both of these questions is a resounding YES! You have miracle working power flowing through you, because the Holy Spirit is alive and well inside of you. Your spirit man has become joined with the Holy Spirit **(I Cor. 6:17),** and you're a walking source of miracle power. It may seem scary at first. However, believe this about yourself and then take a risk by praying for someone that needs miracle power. One thing is for sure. If you don't believe this power is for you, then you'll never walk in it. I'm here to tell you that you can.

I've had several encounters in my life where the power of God helped someone as a result of me praying for them. Let me encourage you with one in particular. I had a business meeting with an elderly lady who was the owner of a company. I waited in the lobby for her, as directed. At the appointed time of the meeting, she came hobbling out with a noticeable limp. She greeted me in the lobby, and we began to get to know each other. I asked her why she was limping. She told me that one of her knees was injured, and the doctor wanted to do surgery on it. I told her that I would like to pray for her after we discussed business, to which she agreed. She was in noticeable pain, so I suggested we just talk in the lobby and allow her to get off her feet. She thanked me for that and took a seat.

After we talked business, it was time to pray. I told her that I didn't believe there were injured knees in heaven, and that I would invite the heavenly realm to come and invade her knee. I laid a hand on her knee and began to pray. I simply invited God's presence and power into the room. I declared the healing authority of Jesus over her and for the power of heaven to become her reality on earth. The prayer lasted no more than 30 seconds.

Before I could even ask her how she was feeling, she jumped up out of the chair declaring, "He healed me, He healed me!" She started walking around her office, declaring her healing to the office staff. There was so much joy and excitement in the moment that it turned into a little party of celebration. Joy in the Holy Spirit is a natural part of God's Kingdom. **(See Romans 14:17)** I think we need more of it. God's Presence is not limited to geography or time. He can release His power anytime and anywhere, and He can do it through you.

Kingdom Connection Thought

Become aware of the exceeding greatness of His power, as you start your first move from the top in the downswing. As you increase the hinging action of your wrists, take ownership of the power that the Holy Spirit has made available to you as a believer. As your right elbow folds closer to your right side, visualize Jesus resting right next to you in the moment. As you do this, know that you're storing up a tremendous amount of power to be released upon the kingdom of darkness. Finally, know that you're powerful in life because the Word says that you are.

Chapter 11
The Continued Assault

Let's continue the downswing, generating a powerful attack angle into the golf ball. Recall that we're in the process of flattening the shaft in order to regain the original, flatter plane. Your hands are continuing to pull the handle of the club down. The path of the hands from the top of the backswing continues on a line that will intersect the ground just inside the target line. At this stage in your downswing, your hands will be below the waist and at the top of your right thigh. (See the picture on the next page.)

Notice in the picture that the hands are slightly higher than the original plane line. This is true of almost every great player on tour. Notice, I stated I want your hands *slightly higher* than the original plane. I don't want your hands too high to the plane line. This will deliver the club on too steep of an angle into impact.

The club shaft is continuing to flatten as we come to this stage. It's through this region that the club head starts to regain the original plane line as it shallows on the way down. Actually, I prefer to see the club head travel slightly underneath, or inside, the original plane. You can shallow the shaft too much and have it drop too far underneath the plane. This can cause the club to *bottom out* early and result in hitting the ground before the ball. This is commonly referred to as a *fat shot*. If you deliver the club from too far underneath the plane, it can also result in a push or hook. Regardless, the desired club face angle is just slightly underneath the plane.

Let me build upon this last statement. You have most likely heard the phrase *swing from the inside out*. Within this phrase, the word *inside* refers to the path of the club head coming from the inside of the original swing plane. I prefer this shaft and club head angle. I believe it's the most consistent angle of attack into the ball in order to gain a solid impact position and ball flight. It's also the most common path utilized by PGA Touring Professionals throughout the decades.

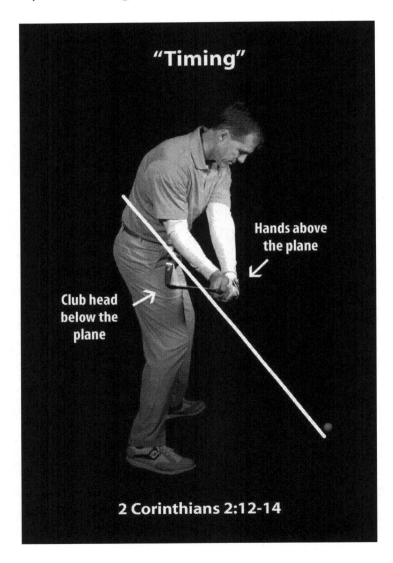

As you look at this picture, you'll see that club head is below the plane line and the hands are above it. This position is one shared by most of the great players. This position is also accompanied by the right elbow continuing to stay tucked in close to the right side underneath the left forearm. If you allow the right elbow to stick out away from your side, the shaft will come down on a steep plane into the ball. As you already know, this is a difficult angle from which to produce good shots. So, having the shaft come down on an angle that passes through your right forearm is highly desirable.

The picture from the front reveals that the shaft is still angled upward. (See next page.) It hasn't yet reached a parallel position relative to the ground, and the club head is still higher than the hands. The *Holy Spirit* (your hands) is still maintaining some hinge in the wrists, reserving the power for the strike into the golf ball. This is a very good position to be in. If your shaft is angled down towards the ground, and the club head is lower than your hands, unfortunately, this is a sign of the casting motion described earlier. The release of the wrist hinge is too early. The timing related to releasing the angle of the shaft is crucial for hitting solid shots.

What about God's timing? It's not the easiest to discern in life. Some people *crash forward* in their plans for God. Despite their best intentions, God wasn't ahead of them, and things didn't work out as planned. In fact, I've seen many times that God didn't open the door for them at all. **Isaiah 30:1** is a clear warning against this type of approach. "'Woe to the rebellious children, 'says the Lord, 'who take counsel, but not of Me, and who devise plans, but not of My Spirit. That they may add sin to sin.'" Ouch! Adding sin upon sin certainly doesn't work out well because it's rooted in rebellion.

Many times, we *go for it* in the name of Jesus, not paying attention to the true intentions of our hearts. These intentions can too often be motivated by selfishness or insecurities. I know that has been true in my life. More than once, I've had a lot of good desires for God's Kingdom in my pursuits. However, when I got really quiet and honest within myself, I knew I was being motivated by an insecurity or fear. God, out of His heart of love and great wisdom, doesn't open the doors that He knows will be destructive to us.

He's too good to do that. Some people get frustrated with God because their plans aren't working out in their timing. Rather, they should ask God what He may be trying to work out in their lives, in His timing.

Some people wait too long and miss their opportunities. They keep trying to figure out every detail of their project and never take the first step to accomplishing their goals. Have you ever met people that talk about what they're going to do for God's Kingdom yet never do more than talk about it? The ministry they're going to start, the mission trip they're going to take or the book they're going to write never comes to fruition. They have all the reasons why they didn't do it and feel like they're utilizing wisdom in the process. However, what they're considering to be wisdom is really a mask for the fear they're operating out of. Sometimes you have to stop waiting for every detail to line up and just go for it. Don't forget that faith is spelled R-I-S-K.

So, what is the balance between going too fast and waiting too long? How do you know if you're moving forward with God's timing in the things of life? Consider Paul's words in **2 Corinthians 2:12**. "Furthermore, when I came to Troas to preach Christ's gospel, and a door was opened to me by the Lord..."

This is a crucial moment in Paul's ministry. He'd intentionally traveled to the region of Troas to preach Christ's gospel. The question is why did he travel to Troas? Because, "a door was opened to me by the Lord." The door was an opportunity for Paul that he could pass through or decline. The key to Paul's statement is found in the phrase *by the Lord*. Paul knew that the Lord was ahead of him and making the opportunity available for him to preach the Gospel in Troas. The Bible doesn't tell us how he knew that the Lord was opening this door to him. We're not informed of a dream or vision, a message from a prophet or the voice of God breaking through in an audible voice. We simply don't know how God communicated with Paul. One thing we know for sure is that Paul was certain the door was opened by the Lord. If he wasn't convinced, he certainly never would've gone.

There are a couple of points I want to make here. First, Paul's schedule was totally interruptible. When Paul was certain that the Lord had opened the door for him go minister in Troas, he made plans to be there. He knew he had to go. Being interruptible for the work of the Kingdom is a valuable attribute to have in your life.

Second, Paul stayed so *in tune* to the promptings of the Holy Spirit that he didn't miss the opportunity that came his way. He walked so closely with the Lord that he knew the voice of His King. It was unmistakable to him, and he acted upon it quickly. Do you walk around with your radar up, tuning in to the frequency of God's communications? Oh, to be more aware of His presence! Oh, to be steadfast upon following the leading of His voice. This is what makes the Lord's timing work clearly in your life. This is when you know whether you're being released or held back by His promptings. This is when dependence and surrender merge into a life that's laid down before the One. We see the result of this combination in **2 Corinthians 2:14**, which gives a clear summary. You're always led in triumph in Christ, diffusing the fragrance of His knowledge wherever you go. Now that is a good way to live life.

Kingdom Connection Thought

The timing in which you allow your wrists to release the hinge of the shaft in the downswing motion is of absolute importance. In the trinity triangle, your wrists are likened to the Holy Spirit. Stay in tune with the Holy Spirit as you work on the proper shaft angles in your attack towards the golf ball. Have some fun with this. If you're releasing the shaft angle too early, tell the Holy Spirit you're sorry for forcing the club out of sequence. Stop taking over in your own strength. If you're lagging the shaft angle behind too long, seek instead to engage the Holy Spirit's release of power sooner. Through it all, stay in tune with the promptings of the One who has great opportunities for your life. He'll see to it that you're always being led triumphantly.

Chapter 12
The Moment of Truth

I've entitled this chapter The Moment of Truth because it's dealing with the hitting zone and the delivery of the club into the golf ball at impact. It doesn't matter how good someone swings the club throughout the backswing and the majority of the downswing. If their mechanics aren't good at the moment they strike into the ball, the results will be disappointing at best. The opposite is also true. There have been many great players that don't have the greatest backswing, and their downswing move has some flaws in it. However, they have an incredible ability to *make it right* as they strike through the ball. They also learned how to repeat this under pressure and win tournaments. At the end of the day, impact is the moment of truth. It determines how well and in what direction the golf ball will fly. .

I think it's safe to say that we all have *continual moments of truth* in our lives. Typically, they happen daily, and they have varying degrees of impact on ourselves and our surroundings. Here are some examples. Despite having good intentions, the tone you use in your voice will have a direct impact on your conversations. It'll also affect the person you're talking with. Another one is the poor health choices people make over a long period of time. After years of bad choices, a doctor tells them of a disease that is taking their life away. That is a moment of significant impact. There are many other examples that could be shared, revealing the *moments of truth that take place in our* lives. Let's remember this as we get back to golf.

In the last chapter, we established a shaft angle that is descending through your right forearm. The wrists are still maintaining some hinge of the club as your hands reach the top of your right thigh. I discussed how these positions relate to the original plane and why they give you a great opportunity to produce great golf shots. Now, it's time to unleash the power on the golf ball. Let's examine impact.

There are some important facts that need to be achieved in order to deliver a solid hit to the golf ball. These facts are what'll cause a ball to fly high, straight and long. I'm going to separate them out individually in order to expound upon them accordingly. The work that you've done from the top of the backswing and the first two positions on the way down have set you up for a beautiful attack angle into the ball. As you can see in the picture below, the hands come into the impact zone a little above the original plane line.

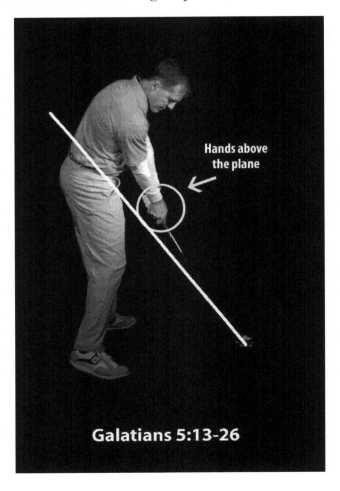

Hands above
the plane

Galatians 5:13-26

The club head is slightly below the original plane. While some of the great players have the club head tracking right down the plane line into the ball, most of them deliver it slightly below.

Notice the angles of the hips and shoulders at impact. The hips are pointing to the right of target. If you could extend a straight line from your belly button, you'd notice that it's pointing to the right of the desired target line. The shoulders are relatively square at impact, so you could also see it as the shoulders remaining parallel to the target line. I point this out to you because it's important to maintain these body angles in order to deliver the club head and shaft into the ball as described. As soon as your shoulders open and point to the left of parallel, and your hips rotate too much through impact, you'll almost certainly produce a steep shaft angle at impact.

When the hips and shoulders rotate too fast in correlation to the shaft and club head, you lose the synchronization of how they work together. The club starts lagging behind the body rotation, which results in a loss of power. While I don't want you to shut down the body rotation, I don't want you to be too quick with your hips and shoulders either. The best way to check this is to video your swing from your right side. Most teachers refer to this as *down the line*. From this angle, you'll clearly see if you need to make adjustments to your hips and shoulders.

Now, take a look at the picture below as we examine the impact position from *face on*. (See the next page.) One of the most imperative realities in order to consistently hit a solid golf ball is to have the *Holy Spirit* (your hands) leading forward of the club head at impact. Some teachers refer to this as having *firm hands*. In the picture, you can see that the hands are clearly ahead of the golf ball as the strike is occurring. If you drop a line straight down from the back of the left hand to the ground, you can see that the line hits the ground in front of the golf ball. The hands leading at impact are absolutely crucial to becoming a good golfer. Great players have utilized many different ways to swing the club back and through. However, when you examine their swings at impact, leading hands are a common denominator you find in all the greats.

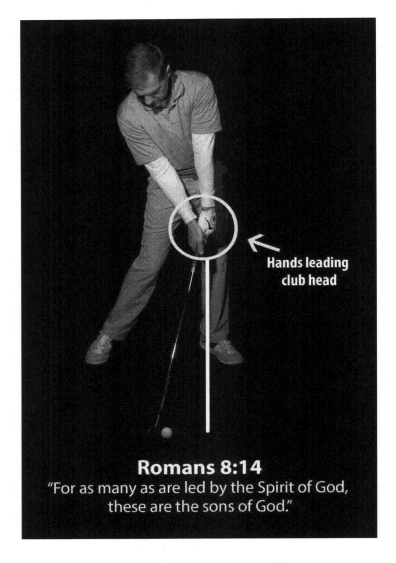

Hands leading club head

Romans 8:14
"For as many as are led by the Spirit of God, these are the sons of God."

Consider the impact position from a few different perspectives. If you were to do a video analysis on how you hit different objects with a stick of some kind, you'd find that the handle is in front of the end of the stick at impact. This is because the hands are leading at the point of contact. This is true whether you're chopping a tree down with an axe or hitting a ball with a baseball bat. The most powerful contact is made when the hands are leading.

I love to teach students how to deliver the hands ahead of the club head in a short chip shot around the green. As we solidify this position in a short shot, I then teach them how to transfer it into longer swings. I frequently tell students that the full swing is a *long* chip shot with full body rotation and a longer arm swing with more wrist action. When that light bulb comes on in their brain, it's been amazing to see the results that have been achieved. They transfer the feeling at impact in the short chip to that of the full swing, and the quality of their ball striking increases dramatically.

The opposite of the hands leading the club head is the club head leading the hands. Unfortunately, this is one of the most common errors I see with amateurs. In this scenario, the back of the left hand breaks down, and the wrists are angled. Inevitably, the left elbow is bending and breaking down with it. Within the golfing trinity triangle, the *Father* and *Holy Spirit* aren't working together in a solidified way and the triangle is falling apart. I joke with people by telling them that this impact position is clearly full of sin and lacking unity amongst the Godhead. It is a joke but holds the truth that this method is not good! This method delivers a weak blow into the golf ball, and the club face angle is typically opening up through impact. This adds loft to the face angle and usually produces a slice. This breakdown of the hands and left arm through impact can also cause the clubface to close too fast and produce a severe pull or hook to the left of your target. When the left hand breaks down, the right hand can easily take over and close the face too fast. As you can tell, this isn't what you want to do as you strike the ball. This method clearly needs some deliverance!

A great tool you can use to overcome this problem is called The Impact Bag. It's a large, vinyl bag that I fill with towels and blankets. When using it, you simply take your club back and strike into the bag. Because it's such a large object, your brain inherently knows that it would be painful to strike the bag without your hands leading. One great truth about humans is that we seek to avoid pain. Therefore, you'll hit into the bag with your hands leading, producing a solid impact position. The key is to transfer this into the *real shot* when hitting a little golf ball. You can find this teaching aid online, and it's truly a great help to many. The bottom line is that you need to have your hands leading the club head into impact. It's one of those non-negotiables with respect to becoming a good golfer.

In the trinity triangle, the *Holy Spirit* relates to our hands. I've clearly hammered the point of letting your hands lead the club head into impact. Let's now relate this impact position to being led by the Holy Spirit. As a child of God, being led by the Spirit should be a normal part of the Christian walk. **Romans 8:14** states this clearly with the words, "For all who are being led by the Spirit of God, these are the sons of God." This also includes His daughters! You can look at this verse another way. If you're a child of God then you're being led by the Spirit of God.

Being led is likened to *being brought forth*. Jesus was led as a sheep to the slaughter. **(See Acts 8:32)** They brought Him forth in order to crucify Him, but it was only because Jesus submitted Himself to this path. He had full authority to stop the Roman guards if He'd wanted to. When Jesus was betrayed and arrested in Gethsemane, He let it be known that He could've stopped the whole process. **Matthew 26: 47-56** tells of an amazing encounter in which we learn of Jesus' total commitment to seeing the Father's will fulfilled. **Verse 53** reveals a powerful question from Jesus. "Or do you think that I cannot now pray to My Father, and He will provide Me with more than twelve legions of angels?" A legion in the Roman military was comprised of 5,000 men. Jesus was letting them know that He could have a minimum of 60,000 angels sent to His aid if He chose. That's a lot of heavenly power. I'm sure these angels were just waiting for the command, so they could have ended the entire incident Jesus was facing. One angel would've been enough. 60,000 angels would have changed the landscape dramatically. Jesus knew this yet didn't *make the call* by praying to His Father for help.

The point is that Jesus allowed Himself to be led to the cross. He was fully committed to seeing the Scripture fulfilled, and the will of the Father done. Jesus perfectly modeled a life being led by God. Whether He was being led by the Spirit to go into the wilderness to be tempted by the devil or to wait for the right moment of time to reveal who He was, Jesus only followed the leading of His Father's Spirit. He modeled this for you and me so that we can do the same. It's important to know that you can.

Being led by the Holy Spirit starts and ends with surrender! What a joyful surrender it truly is. Simply put, if you aren't being led by the Holy Spirit, then you're being led by your flesh. The flesh is your selfish lusts and desires. **Galatians 5: 13-26** breaks down this battle between the Spirit and the flesh beautifully. There simply is no grey area. It's one or the other. The surrender to the Holy Spirit yields the incredible fruit of the Spirit found in **verses 22-23**. A detailed study of the fruit of the Spirit is well worth your time. While I'll not go into great detail on it, I will point out that love is mentioned first for good reason. If you can live by the motto of *let love lead*, chances are real good that you'll be led by the Holy Spirit. The rest of the fruit of the Spirit will easily follow, and your life will be free from the bondages of the law. This is what you were made for. This is what He paid for.

Kingdom Connection Thought

Build your impact position upon your relationship with the Holy Spirit. If you're are not letting your hands lead the club head into impact, then your wrists are breaking down, and you won't consistently deliver a solid strike upon the golf ball. If you're not letting the Holy Spirit lead you in your life, then you'll break down in many areas. Therefore, relate to the Holy Spirit as you're hitting into the impact zone and enjoy the results of His leading. As you do so, be honest with the Lord regarding the areas where you're not being led by His Spirit. Pray right now and let Him speak to you. He will make your paths straight both on and off the golf course.

The next point I want to make with respect to the impact position is the need to hit down into the golf ball. Physics tells us that a ball rises when it's influenced by backspin. Backspin is what makes a golf ball fly up into the air. Topspin makes a ball go down. Topspin is great for tennis but terrible for golf shots. You definitely want backspin imparted to your golf ball as you hit through impact.

Backspin is achieved by the club head striking down into the ball. When done correctly, the club face makes contact with the ball and *traps the ball* between itself and the ground. If you slow down a shot at impact and focus closely on the golf ball, you'll clearly see that the club face makes contact with the ball first. Contact with the ground is made second. You'll also see the ball lifting up into the air before the divot is taken out of the ground. If you hit the ground first and the ball second, you won't produce as solid of a strike. There are also grooves built into the club face, which slightly grab the golf ball during the moment of contact. As the ball is coming off the club face and jumps up off the ground, it'll have backspin on it and fly up in the air. This is what you want. It's a result of the club head hitting down.

The opposite is also true. If the club head swings up into the golf ball, the leading edge of the club is that which will make contact with the ball. The leading edge is at the very bottom of the club face. It doesn't have the flat surface and grooves associated with it, as you find on your club face. If your club head comes in *too high* at impact and strikes the ball with the leading edge, you'll place topspin on the ball. This will produce a shot that runs along the ground, and it won't turn out very well for you.

Golf is a game of opposites. If you want the ball to go up, you'll have to swing the club head down. Take a look back at the picture at impact from the front view. You'll notice how straight the left arm remains going into the impact zone. I mentioned in an earlier chapter that there is a slight, downward flexing of the knees as you enter the hitting area. While the left leg will straighten and *post* at the point of contact, it'll help to be aware of some flex in both legs as you start your downswing. A straight left arm combined with this knee action are key factors in delivering the club head with a downward strike into the ball. You also need to be able to achieve the feeling of the club striking down into the ball and ground, which is related to your hand-eye coordination.

I sometimes have my students make their club head impact the ground during a practice swing. This helps give the necessary sensory feedback they need in order to repeat the feeling in the real swing. There are times when you have to exaggerate this in order to truly achieve a club head that pinches down into the ground at impact. I always recommend working on this with a short chip shot first. Start with a small shot and work your way into the bigger swing. This taps into the Kingdom Principle of *faithful with little, faithful with much.*

There are many reasons why a golfer struggles with creating this solid impact position. One of the most common is their left arm and wrist break down and fold. This shortens the arm, which in turn pulls the club up from the ground and ball. It's hard to hit down when your arm and club are pulling up. There's a great training aid called the Straight Arm, which helps overcome this problem. It's like a cylinder that wraps around your left arm with the elbow in the center of the device. It doesn't allow you to bend your left arm while swinging, which should help you produce a downward attack into the ball. I've also seen many golfers lift their chest and head too quickly while trying to hit into the ball. This raises their spine angle and typically produces a *topped shot.*

In conjunction with this, many golfers straighten up their legs quickly and have a jumping motion as they come into impact. While there are some great players that do this, keep in mind they have to maintain a forward tilt in their spine angle at the same time. It's very hard for the average golfer to jump up with their legs while keeping their chest angled down. At the same time, they need to keep their arms extended as they rotate their body and hit into a golf ball. That's a lot to manage within a split second of time. The exception doesn't need to become the rule. At the end of the day, you need to achieve a club head that is hitting down before the golf ball will fly up.

Down before up! There's so much truth in these three words. Before there can be resurrection, there must first be death. Jesus had to go into the grave before He could ascend to the Father. Lazarus had to die and be placed in the tomb before Jesus could glorify the Father by raising him from the dead. **(See John 11)** There is clearly an order to these events. Death precedes resurrection. Let's take a closer look at **Matthew 16: 24-25** where Jesus states, "If anyone desires to come after Me, let him deny himself, and take up his cross, and follow Me. For whoever desires to save his life will lose it, and whoever loses his life for My sake will find it." On a quick side note, I always find it humorous when I hear people declare that the Bible was written by man. This point usually comes out when someone is debating Christianity. Let me assure you that *dying to self* and *taking up your cross* are not themes you ever hear from a humanistic perspective. The nature of the flesh is selfish, arrogant and protective. Man wrote the Bible for his own purposes? I don't' think so. Let get back to the Scripture.

There are several points here that can be studied out in great detail. I encourage you to do so. Jesus' statement starts with, "If anyone desires to come after Me." This isn't a command. This is an invitation. This choice is undergirded by a personal desire, which is rooted in your will. However, there are specific conditions Jesus communicates if you choose to follow Him. You must deny yourself and take up your cross. These conditions require you to disown yourself to the point where you've died to the old ways of life you once lived. The old ways you lived before looking into the eyes of the One who's pure love. Once you have experienced that, the things of earth truly do grow strangely dim, in the light of His glory and grace. Losing your life for His sake is a wonderful thing, knowing that the end result is actually finding the life He has for you.

As said before, there must first be death before there can be resurrection. There is a grave of the soul that you must go into. Jesus, who is the resurrection, knows what He's doing. When He who is the resurrection calls you to first die, it's because He knows that you will take flight into the resurrection life He has for you. He didn't stay on the cross or in the grave, and He doesn't intend for you to either. He intends for you to live in the power of the resurrection. Therefore, don't go back and occupy the grave (old life) you've been resurrected from. When the old is gone, it is gone. When the new has come, it has come. Believe it and live it. In His Kingdom, life on this earth is Easter Sunday every day. Go ahead and die to the things of this world. Resurrection life is so much better!

Kingdom Connection Thought

Your club head needs to dig a grave by taking a divot as you strike through the golf ball. Hit down enough to get the club face on the ball at impact. You'll impart backspin on the ball and watch it soar up into the air. Visualize Jesus going into the grave and then resurrecting fully triumphant over death. Death in Christ leads to resurrection victory. Therefore, connect your heart into this victory as you drive your club head through impact. Be confident that the shallow grave you dig will yield great heights. The ball will fly high and so will you.

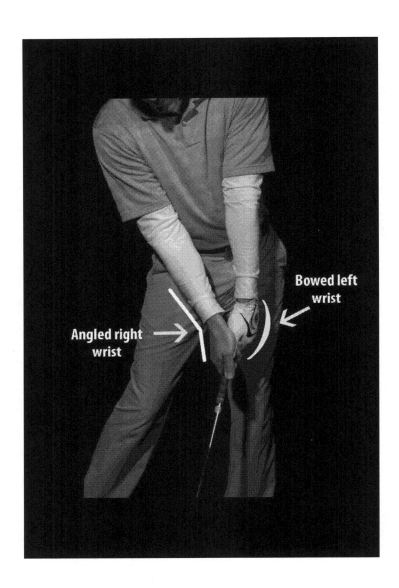

Chapter 13
The Release

As the club comes into impact from the attack angle I've been teaching, the club face should be a few degrees open. This means it's pointing slightly to the right (between one and four degrees) of the target. Therefore, there is a need to release the club face through the hitting zone. If you don't, the club face will remain open and the ball will fly to the right of the target. The release is also referred to as rotating or squaring the club face. It's important for you to know that I prefer a ball flight that has a slight draw to it. For the right-handed golfer, this means the ball will curve in the air from right to left. I like to see the ball start out a bit to the right of your target (typically three to six yards) and curve back towards the target in the air. In addition, I *don't* want to see the ball draw to the left of the target line, which I refer to as *crossing the line*.

The release of the club face at impact within the first foot or two after the strike, will place a slight right-to-left spin on the golf ball. This is what makes it curve (or draw) to the left in the air. The question is: what is the most effective way to release the club face through impact? This is a good question. Recall that I want to see your hands leading the club head into impact. In conjunction with this, I prefer to see the back of your left hand with a slight bow to it as you hit through the ball. You can see this in the picture on the previous page. This means there will be a rounded curve to the back of the hand. Other phrases teachers use to describe this position are *turning the hand down* or *knuckling down*.

Tiger Woods is famous for the *stinger shot* he used so successfully to win the British Open and many other tournaments. Tiger clearly utilizes the bowed left hand position in order to hit the stinger shot. There will be a slight bend in your left wrist. The back of your left hand will feel like it's angled towards the ground. In order to achieve this position of the left hand, the right wrist will have to bend in the opposite way. You'll actually keep your right wrist angled back.

Now, here's a big key in order to achieve the release of the clubface in the midst of this move. As your left wrist is bowing, and your right wrist is angled back, both hands are participating in rotating down and to the left. This rotating motion is what turns the clubface from a slightly open position towards a square one. Please note that the clubface doesn't need to be dead square in the brief moment that the golf ball is in contact with the club face. Some refer to this as *zeroing out*. Rather, as the club face is rotating inward a few degrees, this is the release that imparts the slight sidespin from right to left. The path of the club head partners in with the hand action I'm describing, to produce a drawing flight pattern. I know I'm using very technical language right now. However, stay focused with me. This is an important concept for you to grasp.

Please recall my teaching earlier in the book in regards to the rounded centrifugal force generated in the golf swing. This is achieved in part by the rotational motion of the hips and shoulders. Also, the pathway of the club head is clearly more rounded than linear. When you combine these together, there's a significant amount of rotational force that effects the release of the club face through impact. This is why I prefer the leading of the hands with a slightly bowed left wrist through impact. It minimizes the amount of face movement in the club head.

If you add extra club face rotation by flipping your right hand over your left, you're creating a very inconsistent and untrustworthy club face angle in your swing. Sure, you can hit some really solid shots this way if you time this flipping motion at impact really well. Yes, I know there are some world class players that have *flippy hands* through impact. And, yes, I know there's a popular theory out there that teaches this method will help you hit the ball really far. Regardless, I firmly believe that the more you can minimize the rotation of the club face through the hitting area, the more consistent you'll strike the ball. Did you pick up on the word *consistent* in the last sentence? Consistency is what wins golf tournaments. I also believe it'll help you achieve a more repeatable ball flight you can trust. A trusted flight pattern partnered with making a lot of putts is also what wins golf tournaments. What is the bottom line? Don't be a *flipper of the hands* to release the club face through impact.

Shaft parallel to the ground

Posting the left leg

Let's keep moving through the hitting area into the next stage of the golf swing. It should read, "as you can see in the picture on the previous page, the hands have reached the waist high position. The club shaft has achieved a parallel relationship to the ground. Also, notice how the left leg has straightened. This is what I referred to in Chapter 6 when I discussed posting your left leg. The posting of the left leg plays a part in allowing the hips to continue rotating to the finish position. This is a reminder because I don't want you to forget how the hands, arms and club work in conjunction with the body rotation.

You also see how the right forearm is still underneath the left forearm. This is a result of releasing the club face with the bowed left wrist as previously discussed. Some of you are thinking, "I've been taught to rotate my right forearm over my left forearm through impact my whole life." I understand. I also understand that there are times when a player needs to feel the forearm rotation activated in their swing in order to release the club face at all. Some players need that to stop the club face from staying open on every swing. However, if you depend upon a lot of forearm rotation, you'll risk having excessive club face rotation and hooking the ball. There is a subtle amount of rotation in the right forearm as you establish a bowed left wrist through the hitting zone. I think you will find a healthy balance as you work on this. Ultimately, I'm steering you away from using flippy hands and aggressive forearm rotation to release the club face. The right forearm staying under the left forearm is a good sign that you're not a flipper. Remember, Flipper is a dolphin not a golfer!

Look at the extension of both the right and left arms at this stage. Within the trinity triangle, the *Father, Son* and *Holy Spirit* have unleashed a mighty blow upon the head of the enemy. The acceleration that accompanies this blow results in this extension. All three members of the *Trinity* are working together in unison and are extending the club towards the target. This is my speculation, but I like to think of the excitement existing within the Trinity at this stage. The devil has been totally caught off guard, and his defeat has been made complete through the Cross and Resurrection of Christ. The wisdom, omniscience and pure power of the Father have rendered the enemy helpless and broken.

Back to golf. With this extension comes the maximum amount of club head speed. This speed, combined with a solid delivery of the club head through impact, results in tremendous power. As I swing through impact into this position of extended arms, I like to imagine the joy in Heaven as the power of God dismantled the enemy's plans. It also encourages me to generate the maximum amount of speed as my club head travels through impact into this position.

If you're not experiencing the extension of the arms and the club head speed you desire, you're probably breaking down the left arm and wrist as you hit through the ball. This is a classic problem I see with many golfers; especially those that come into impact from an outside angle. When you see it on video, it's not a pretty site. The *Father* (left elbow) and Son (right elbow) are bent and pulled up into the body. *The Holy Spirit* (hands) have also broken down. The momentum of the club head is being lost. The arms are shortening instead of extending away from the body. Again, if you deliver the club head into the ball from a steep angle that is outside the plane, you'll be prone to breaking down the hands and arms through the hitting zone. This is because the arms are swinging back into the body at this point. The body gets in the way and something has to give. It's usually the arms bending and collapsing.

If this is you, I'd first recommend working to achieve a flatter shaft angle on the downswing. This will put you into a much better position to extend your arms through impact. I already mentioned a training aid called The Straight Arm. This can help you at this stage in the golf swing as well. Maintaining extension in the arms as you hit into an Impact Bag is another good way to work out this problem. You'll feel your triceps muscles tightening in order to stabilize the left arm and keep it straight. It'll take some effort, but you can do it. .

Now, I want to focus on the pathway of the hands, shaft and club head, relative to the original plane line. As you examine the picture below, you'll notice that the hands, shaft and club head are slightly to the right of the original plane line.

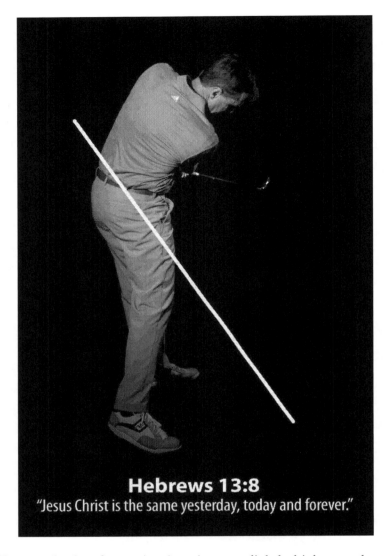

Hebrews 13:8
"Jesus Christ is the same yesterday, today and forever."

Due to the hands coming into impact slightly higher to the plane, combined with the extension of the arms and the centrifugal force acting upon the pathway, the club is slightly outside the plane at this point. This is why you hear some teachers using the phrase *swing from inside to out*. There are fine lines to this phrase, but it should make sense within the context of what I'm teaching.

It's important to note that the path of the shaft and club head are still moving in sync with the body rotation. If the body rotation stops entirely, the hands will likely break down due to the momentum of the club head. The path of the club is still curving in a rounded direction, moving *up and in* relative to the plane. Notice in the picture from the front how the shaft has regained a parallel relationship to the ground and target line. These parallel lines, partnered with a square club face, reveal a golf ball that'll be flying towards your desired target. The golf ball has been struck at this point. However, achieving this position is a great sign that your club has passed through impact in a most productive way.

Consistent! This is the word I emphasized earlier in the chapter with respect to the club face angle as it travels through impact. Yet, when you consider this word in context of the Lord, it embodies a joyful trust. It's a happy thought. It's solid and good. **Hebrews 13:8** declares, "Jesus Christ is the same yesterday, today and forever." Jesus is the same! He is entirely of Himself and likened to no other. He is totally complete within His own makeup. He doesn't need to take on the attributes of another. He never has and never will. Perfection doesn't need any help. This is why He's unchanging and utterly consistent.

When someone is inconsistent, you're not sure if you can trust them. If they have major mood swings or react differently to you from moment to moment, you quickly learn to protect yourself from them. Business leaders who don't have consistent ethics and standards will repeatedly change the rules for their own benefit. Children are greatly frustrated by parents who aren't consistent in their parenting approaches. They learn to be unsure of what to expect from Mom and Dad, which isn't a safe place for children to be. There are many other examples that could be stated, but t. he bottom line is most people keep healthy boundaries from people who produce challenging inconsistencies. This is sometimes necessary and perfectly OK. Boundaries are permissible.

This is not Jesus, though! You can trust Jesus because He'll never change on you. Because He is love, you'll never stop being loved. It's worth stating again. You'll never stop being loved! Because He's the prince of peace, you'll never have a lack of peace. Because He's truth, you'll never have to question if He's lying to you. Because He's full of mercy, you'll never have to wake up doubting if there are fresh mercies for you that morning. Because He's good, you'll never have to doubt His intentions towards you and for you. Because He's holy, you'll always have a reason to worship Him.

The list could go on and on. I love Paul's choice of words in **Ephesians 3:8** when he writes, "that I should preach among the Gentiles the unsearchable riches of Christ." He's saying the riches of Christ are so expansive that you can't even track them. These riches are too vast and enormous to map out. Yet, in the midst of the unsearchable riches, He's simply unchanging. The more you discover about Him, the more you realize He always has been, and will forever be, the same. This is why you can trust and follow Jesus in all His ways. You can trust His voice and the direction He speaks to you. He really is this good.

Kingdom Connection Thought

Jesus is consistent. He's unchanging. Remember this as you're striking the golf ball at impact. Tell the Holy Spirit you are going to let Him lead you through the hitting zone. Connect into Him as you feel your hands leading the club face as you hit the ball. If your hands break down and flip through impact, just repent and assure the Holy Spirit you'll do better on the next swing. You may laugh at that thought, but that is real communion. That type of connection is abiding in the Vine. I believe the Lord loves it. Envision a club face that's not quickly, changing direction as it's swinging through the ball. Relate this to the consistency of Jesus yesterday, today and forever. May all of this result in a golf ball that is struck solidly and flies on a great line towards your target.

Chapter 14
The Finish Position
(A Place of Rest)

We're almost home. I've worked through many parts of the swing with you. It's now time to cross the finish line and complete the golf motion. Let's get after it. In general, there are many different finish positions. Some of the greatest players of all time have positions at the top of their finish that are quite unique. Arnold Palmer comes to mind with his left elbow flying out to the side, and the shaft crossing back over his head. Some players have very short, abbreviated finishes. Some refer to this as a *sawed off* three quarter finish. Some would argue that because the golf ball has already been hit, it doesn't really matter how you finish. There may be some truth to that. However, in order to complete the mechanical approach I've been teaching you, I believe there are some important points in order to finish well.

Don't forget that we've been building the action of the arms, hands and club upon the rotation of the body. This principle doesn't change as we come to our resting position at the finish. The rotation of the hips and shoulders must continue all the way to our stopping point. This is due to the momentum and force being exerted through the shaft and club head. They don't want to stop at the halfway point. Therefore, continuing the body rotation is crucial. If you stop rotating halfway to the top, you'll be forced to collapse your arms and hands, draping them over your left shoulder and into your chest. The trinity triangle would fall apart, which isn't good.

Take a look at the picture on the next page. In examining the body rotation, you can see how straight the left leg is. The left leg is the solid post upon which most of the body weight is now balanced. The right

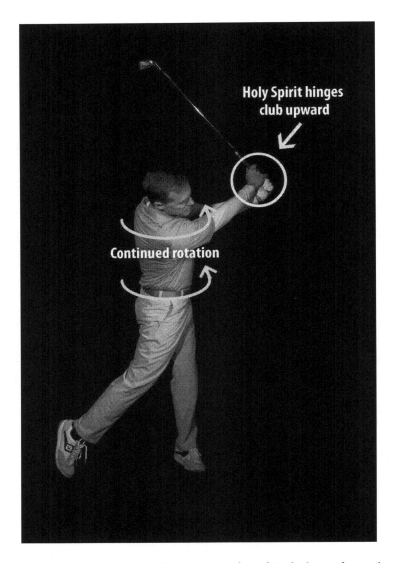

foot has come completely off the ground and is balanced on the toe. This is the result of a full hip rotation to the finish. The shoulders have continued to rotate all the way around to the left side of your body. As mentioned earlier in the book, the hips are now pointing at your target while your chest is pointing to the left of target by approximately 35 degrees. This amount of hip and shoulder rotation is what allows your hands and arms to finish high above your head. As the shoulder rotation continues to the left side, this is what enables your hands and arms to finish on the left side of your head. This creates some nice depth at the top of your finish—the same as you achieved at the top of your backswing.

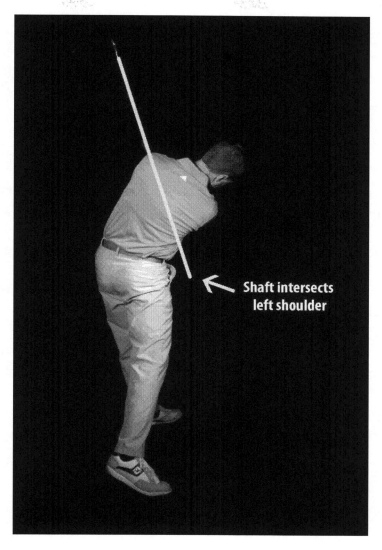

Shaft intersects
left shoulder

Let's take a closer look at the path of the club, and what is happening inside the trinity triangle. As mentioned in the previous chapter, the shaft and club head have swung through impact slightly to the outside of the original plane line. This is due to the path of the club and extension of the arms through the hitting zone. The club head is now traveling from the top of your left thigh in an upwards motion above your head. Simply put, the club head is going to start traveling on a more vertical angle, just as it did halfway through your backswing. We achieved this in the backswing by allowing the *Holy Spirit* (your hands) to hinge the club upward. We'll do it the same way in the follow through.

The *Holy Spirit* is engaged by hinging the club vertically. The club is rotating with your body turn to your finish position. The shaft will typically intersect through the middle of your left shoulder or slightly lower. You can see this in the picture from behind. (See the image on the previous page.) This depends upon how early you start the hinging motion. If you start it earlier, it'll intersect just underneath the left shoulder. If you hold the *bowed left wrist* angle a bit longer through this region, the shaft will intersect a bit higher through the left shoulder. I am fine with either one as long as your shaft is in within this range.

The action of the arms to the finish position can also vary a bit amongst the professionals. However, there are some striking similarities as well. When your hands get to your chest, I want to see both your arms still extended straight. The *Father* (left elbow) and *Son* (right elbow) are working in tandem here to keep the triangle rotating in sync with the body rotation. They are also maintaining the beautiful width you see on the left side of the body.

Let's now go all the way to the top of the forward swing to the finish position. Take a look at these pictures at the top of the forward swing. (See the following three images.) The hips and shoulders have completed their rotational motion. The left leg is still straight. The right knee has come forward and rests a few inches away from the left knee. The hands have reached their full height above your head and to the outside of your left shoulder. At the top of the backswing, you feel your left arm stretching across your chest. You'll now feel your right arm stretching across your chest at the top of the finish as it flows with your shoulder rotation.

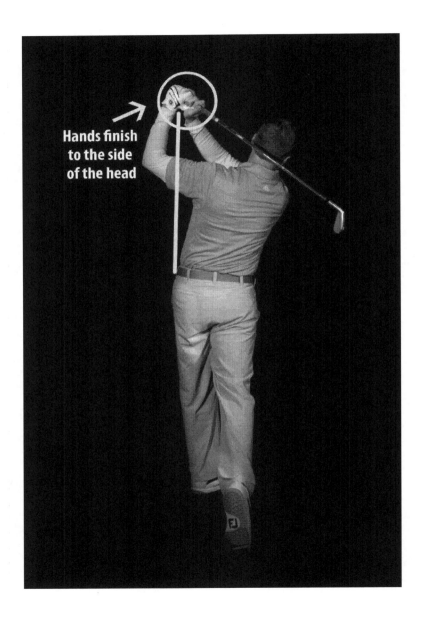

Hands finish to the side of the head

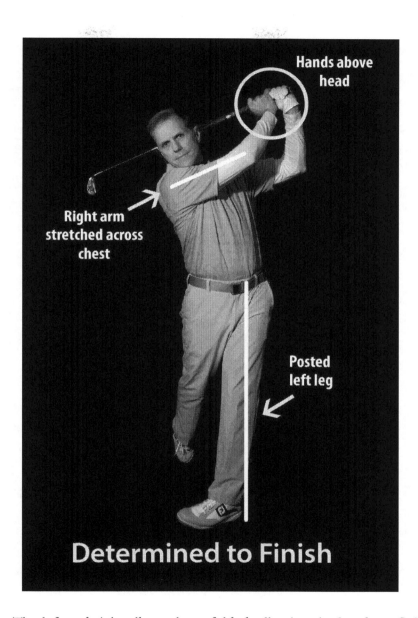

The left and right elbows have folded, allowing the hands to finish behind the head in a comfortable resting position. By folding, the *Father* (left elbow) makes sure He is staying close to your side. *Jesus*

(right elbow) stays close to you in the backswing and most of the downswing. The *Father* continues this on your behalf as the swing comes to its rest at the top.

Some players like to keep the right arm extended a bit straighter than others at the top. This is especially true for the player who keeps their left wrist bowed a long time through impact and utilizes a shorter follow through. However, I like to see the right elbow fold with the left as the arms flow with the shoulder rotation to the top. I relate it to *coming to a place of rest* after unleashing such strength and power through the hitting zone. It's like a *Sabbath moment* where you can rest from your work. You can relax the muscles and enjoy seeing the flight of a beautiful golf shot.

Congratulations! You got there. You did it. You completed the golf swing from start to finish. It hasn't been easy, but you made it. It's a victorious feeling for sure. While this is great to achieve in your golf swing, how much more necessary in your life. Stay focused with me here, as I'm going to share something very important for your life in Christ.

Jesus' last moments of life on the Cross, His finish line as a man, reveal some important truths for us to take hold of. You can find this account in **John 19: 25-30**. He made sure that His mother was taken care of by John. He modeled to us the importance of honoring our parents up to our last moments with them. This is true regardless of who passes on first. In **Verse 28** it states, "After this, Jesus, knowing that all things were now accomplished, that the Scripture might be fulfilled, said 'I thirst.'" Then in **Verse 30** Jesus speaks His last words by saying, "It is finished." I want to draw your attention to the words *accomplished, fulfilled* and *finished*. These are definitive words describing Jesus' last moments and mission on the earth.

Accomplished and *finished* are the exact same Greek word. The word *fulfilled* is a slight variation with a very similar meaning. Synonyms for these words are "to execute," "to complete," "to conclude," and "to be discharged." Through the writing of John—the beloved—the Holy Spirit is making it very clear that Jesus completed every aspect of His purpose and work set for Him to do on this earth. He would never have allowed them to kill Him if it weren't so. Not fulfilling the Father's assignment for Him was not an option. Apply the word *determination* to the lens that you look at Jesus' life through. To the point of death, He was determined to execute every work, conversation, teaching and act He'd set out to do.

What about your purpose? What about your destiny? What about the assignment God has put you on the planet to accomplish? What are you giving yourself to? **Philippians 1:6** declares, "Being confident of this very thing, that He who has begun a good work in you will perform it until the day of Jesus Christ." The word *perform* means "to fulfill or execute." It holds the same meaning as the words used to describe Jesus' work on this planet. The Lord will be faithful see His work in you completed because He was faithful to complete His own work. There is no double standard in operation here. I also believe Paul is building off the phrase in **Verse 5** when he writes to the saints in Philippi, "Your fellowship in the gospel." He's talking about their partnership, or participation, in the advancement of the gospel. Trust me in this. There is a work to be done for the sake of His Kingdom and the Gospel of Christ.

It's of utmost importance for all of us to wrestle with God in order to determine the work that He has for us. By this, I mean a specific calling or work to do according to the gifts, talents and abilities He's given to us. You need to challenge yourself with **Ephesians 2:10** which states, "For we are His workmanship, created in Christ Jesus for good works, which God prepared beforehand that we should walk in them." God has prepared good works for you and me to walk in. And we should walk in them.

This is why I've written this book. I believe it's a part of the good works I'm called to walk in as I live on this earth for His Kingdom. Pray and ask the Lord for clarification on these points. Examine your thoughts, dreams and talents. Ponder the desires you have in your heart for Him. Evaluate what you're naturally drawn to in order to see if God has an open door for you in those areas. Remember, God knows the plans He has for you. He's put His desires in your heart to come alive when you're born again by His Spirit. These are the plans that bring His life out of you.

Psalm 37:4 says it this way, "Delight yourself also in the Lord, and He will give you the desires of your heart." To delight yourself in the Lord is to make yourself moldable in His hands. He's the potter and you're the clay. You're willing to be shaped however He sees fit to mold you. The word *desire* can be broken into *de* and *sire*. *De* means "of." The word *sire* can be defined as *the father that provides the necessary seed for procreation.* Therefore, you can think of the word *desire* as meaning *the seeds that are of the father.* In other words, the Father places seeds from His heart into your heart. As you make yourself moldable, His seeds take root and grow in your heart. You want these seeds to grow in your life for they contain the blueprints of His plans for you. His life is in His seeds. You definitely want His life flourishing in your life.

Therefore, you need to fight for His plans and purposes to come forth in your life. You need an intense determination to do the work necessary to see His plans for your life executed in full. You have to go the distance. You cannot pray for five minutes and walk away thinking, "God must not be doing this in my life." No, pray again—and again if necessary. How long should you pray? As long as it takes. Daniel fasted and prayed for 21 days until he won the victory in the spirit realm. **(See Daniel 10)** Just like Daniel, you will find that it is worth it to pray until you get your breakthrough.

You have to be willing to go through all the seasons of life that'll come your way. This includes the ups and downs. Seasons of joy and those of discouragement. A seed must lie dormant under the ground, packed in the dirt with no sunlight, before is sprouts forth its fruit. Some seeds have longer periods of dormancy than others. That's why you must be determined to never quit on what you believe God has for you. Is God stirring old thoughts and dreams inside you as you're reading this? If so, it's because His seeds inside you never die. Some people quit on God, but He never quits on them. Don't quit. Rekindle the fire for old dreams if necessary. Pray again in faith. Cry out to God for breakthroughs and endure with Him to the end. Get to the finish line of God's dreams inside of you. You are more than a conqueror in Christ. You were designed to overcome obstacles because the great Overcomer lives inside of you. God believes in you. I believe in you. May you get to the end of your life and be able to say, "It was all worth it for the sake of His Kingdom."

Kingdom Connection Thought

See Jesus as the victorious King who executed the Father's plan to completion. Know that He didn't quit but overcame every obstacle in His way. Use this as your motivation to rotate your hips, shoulders, arms and club all the way to your finish position. Don't stop short of the top. Push yourself to new heights in your swing. Work hard in the process of transformation. As you go through life, see yourself the way Jesus sees you. . Connect with the great Overcomer as you rest at the top of your finish position. Enjoy communing with Him as you watch a beautiful shot fly off your club face. The journey is the destiny so enjoy it with Him.

Chapter 15
Rhythm

Breath. Such a simple word with so much importance. We're dependent upon breathing in order to deliver the required oxygen throughout our bodies. Life ceases without it. When you study the word *God*, one of the most basic meanings is "breath." Maybe this is why there's no life without God. This is because He *is* breath and there is no life without breath. This is explained very clearly in **Genesis 2:7** which states, "And the Lord God formed man of the dust of the ground, and breathed into his nostrils the breath of life; and man became a living being." God breathed into a clump of clay and loosed life into it. Adam was the result. Without God's breath of life, humanity wouldn't have come into existence. **2 Timothy 3:16** reminds us that Scripture is God breathed. In **John 20:22**, Jesus breathed on the disciples so they'd receive the Holy Spirit. God's breath is of great importance. .

The average human breathes approximately 20,000 times per day. That's a lot of life flowing in and out of you. Most of us take it for granted, as breathing is a subconscious function. If you're struggling for breath, you don't take it for granted. If you breathe easily, be thankful. None of us are promised to be breathing tomorrow. I appreciate every breath I take.

Have you ever closed your eyes and focused on the rhythm associated with breathing? You feel the air fill up your lungs and then rush back out your mouth. It feels good. I want to focus now on a deep breath. You know, the kind the doctor asks you to take when they're listening to your lungs with a stethoscope. That's the big, deep breath I'm referring to. You breathe in as much air as you can and then let it all out. I like to take this type of breath when the air is cold outside. It's refreshing to my lungs, and it never gets old seeing the vapor come out of my mouth when I exhale.

I want you to consider the tempo associated with this deep breathing. You breathe the air in nice and slow and then breathe out much more rapidly. It feels passive going in and a bit violent going out. Breathe in slow and breathe out fast. When I compare the timing of the two, I sense the breath going out is twice as fast as the breath going in. You could also say that you inhale twice as long as you exhale. What's the point? The point is that I want you to relate this timing to the tempo of your golf swing. The rhythm of the swing is crucial to hitting good golf shots. Maybe that's why I've saved this chapter for last.

If you took a poll of PGA Touring Professionals, asking them the importance of rhythm in their golf swing, I doubt any of them would rank anything more important. While the mechanics of their golf swings vary, tempo is what brings it all together. They're at their best when the rhythm of their back swing and forward swing are beautifully synchronized. When their timing is on, there's no telling how low a score they'll shoot that day. Ask Jim Furyk. He has a very unorthodox golf swing that you would *not* teach. Yet, he holds the record for the lowest score ever shot on the PGA Tour with a 58. Let's not forget that he also shot a 59 in another tournament. His rhythm was, without question, as important as anything working for him on those days. It didn't hurt that he made a ton of putts either.

Here are some thoughts on how to implement tempo within your golf swing. Recall my reference to the timing when you inhale, compared to when you exhale your deep breath. It's essentially twice as long. There's an old drill that's been used by many that I call a *one, two, three tempo drill.* The *one* and *two* relate to your backswing while the *three* relates to your downswing. In your backswing, you count to two. It's not as slow as the classic, *one thousand one, one thousand two* timing used to count the seconds on a clock. It's also not a rushed, fast tempo. If you use a stopwatch, it takes about one second to count to two. That's a pretty good gauge. Before you start the downswing in this drill, I'd like to implement a slight pause. It gives your brain a chance to feel the full rotation of your backswing and gain feedback as to where the club is relative to your body. I'd also like the pause to overcome a tendency to get quick from the top. If you are too quick from the top, you can easily run the risk of getting the shaft too steep on the way down.

As you continue this drill, you achieve *the three* as the club is swinging through the impact zone. This is where you want to pick up your maximum speed. This is another reason why you don't want to be quick from the top. You don't want your maximum speed in the first move down. You want it at the ball and the first three feet in front of impact. When I implement the slight pause at the top, the way I count in my head is likened to *one, two and three.* The two is at the top of the backswing. The *and* is right as I start down from the top. And the *three* is as my club head is traveling through the ball. Give this a try with some practice swings first and then see if you can implement it into a real shot.

A lot of touring pros have utilized a metronome during practice sessions. This helps them keep the tempo they're after. You may want to try this yourself. There's also a Swing Stick on the market that's helpful. It utilizes a very flexible shaft. It requires you to swing with a smooth tempo to accommodate the increased flex. If you swing too fast, the flexible shaft doesn't correlate well.

Here are a few other thoughts for you. Keep the pressure in your hands and arms soft and relaxed. This will help you maintain a smooth tempo. On a side note, it will also aid the hinging of the wrists and folding of the right elbow in the backswing. If you're tense and tight in your hands and arms, the tendency is to speed up the tempo of the golf swing. When you swing too fast, you can easily lose the proper sequencing of the swing coordinated with your body rotation. God is not stressed out and He's not in a hurry. These are good attributes to incorporate into your life and golf swing.

Kingdom Connection Thought

Let God breathe His presence on you as you swing the golf club. Connect to the rhythm of deep breathing as it's taken in and out. Feel the air fill your lungs to full capacity and the power with which it leaves your mouth. Emulate the timing of this deep breathing into the tempo of your golf swing. Don't rush it! Move with God's breath in your life. Let the rhythm of your swing flow with it as well. Stay relaxed and slow so that you don't get ahead of the proper sequencing in the swing. Apply this thought to your current circumstances, so you don't get out of step with the Lord. His timing truly is perfect in all things.

Conclusion

What an amazing journey we've had through the mechanics of the golf swing. We've traveled together from the grip and stance all the way to the finish position. As I'm writing, I feel a lot of gratitude in my heart that you've gone on this journey with me. I know it's been a different approach to the game of golf than you've probably ever been on. I hope I've brought out ideas that have helped you in your walk with the Lord and your walk down the fairways.

I want to end where I began by reminding you of a Kingdom Principle that's foundational to all of life. It comes out of **Acts 17:28a,** which states, "For in Him we live and move and have our being." It all starts with being *in Him*. This is a declaration of our identity in the Lord. You should do a word study on this phrase, or the phrase *in Christ*. You'll be amazed at the declarations made about you in the Scriptures as a son or daughter of the King. If you'll believe and declare them every day, you'll find your life advancing in the ways God designed for you to live in.

Within this Scripture, also lies the reality that we *move in Him*. The golf swing requires movement from start to finish. Therefore, the game of golf qualifies to be played in Christ. It may still seem like a unique concept, but one that I believe is greatly overlooked in Christian teaching. We learn about Jesus but what about doing life in, with and through Him? I believe this is a main reason Jesus came to earth, lived as a perfect model for us to follow, died for our sins, resurrected from the grave and empowered us with the Holy Spirit. All of this for never ending communion and life that is intertwined together.

I've also taken the golf mechanics very seriously in this book. I want you too as well. The golf swing is based upon principles of physics and mathematics. Principles that tap into God's creative genius.

Good mechanics produce good golf shots. I hope that you've learned a lot about golf mechanics and have become more knowledgeable in your overall understanding of the golf swing. I believe this book will help you play your best golf. I want you to play great golf! I hope to hear your testimonies of lowering your personal best scores, winning tournaments and setting course records. You can do it.

Mostly, I truly want you to have the Scripture come to life inside of you so that you can know Jesus in a way you never have. I'm not talking about head knowledge. I'm talking about deep communion with Him. I want you to have such sensitivity to the Holy Spirit and the voice of our Lord that the smallest moments of your day are influenced by Him. Remember, this is the best version of you to be lived out on this planet. You might as well start now.

I'm asking you to take the Kingdom Connection points found at the end of each chapter very seriously. Dig deeper into them. Find other Scriptures that relate to the principles and implement them into your game and life. Have fun with them as you work them out in your golf swing. It takes time to train your brain so that you will incorporate this communion with the Trinity into your mechanics. The more diligently you work on it, the more natural it becomes. As it becomes more natural, it gets simple. I literally hit golf shots by acknowledging Him in my setup, keeping Jesus (right elbow) close to my side in the back swing, and letting the Holy Spirit (my hands) lead intentionally through impact. Although there are many other components to my swing, I hit great shots when I focus on these principles. Yours will be different than mine. You develop your own summary of thoughts related to the points of the book. It's your golf swing. He is your Lord. Make it yours and meet Him in the midst of it all.

Finally, I'm so honored that you would read and learn from me through this book. I pray that God has met you through these pages and that He will meet you on the golf course.

Speaking of prayer, let me conclude by declaring this prayer over you:

"Lord Jesus, I ask that you meet my friend where they are right now. Pour out more of Your love upon them. Enrich their hearts to know You deeply and to understand the fullness of Your heart for them. May the game of golf now become a place of continual fellowship with You. May it become a place of communion. May Your word and voice become clear in the motions of their golf swing. When they hit good shots, may they rejoice with You. When they hit bad shots, may they laugh and learn from You. Let the game of golf become a beautiful walk for them as they play in You, with You and for You. You are worthy of it all. I pray this in the matchless name of Jesus! Amen and amen!"

Many Blessings to you,
Chuck Hammett

About the Author

Golf and ministry are two words that are deeply connected to Chuck Hammett's life. They've gone *hand-in-hand* for more than two decades. Growing up in Venice, Florida, Hammett started playing golf at the age of seven with his father and brother. He played and competed in many sports as a youth before turning his full time attention to golf at the age of thirteen. Under the tutelage of renowned teacher Jim Duval (David Duval's uncle), Hammett developed into one of the top juniors in Florida.

At the age of fifteen, Hammett was the youngest golfer in the state to qualify for the Florida State Amateur, where he successfully made the cut. Chuck qualified for the State Amateur again two years later and has won many junior tournaments in his career. His talents landed him a golf scholarship at Stetson University where he graduated in 1991 with a Bachelor of Science in Chemistry.

Shortly after college, Hammett began his professional career in golf. While he was a good player, he realized that his greatest talent was found in teaching. Hammett began his professional teaching career at the Bill Skelley School of Golf in Niceville, Florida. It was also during this season of life that his walk with God began to go to a higher level.

His life went from having a causal relationship with God to one with ministry purpose for His Kingdom. While his teaching skills were being honed, Chuck received a unique call from the Lord: to write a golf ministry book. He completed this assignment by writing and publishing his first book, *Jesus Would Have Been a Scratch Golfer*. The book had three printings and sold over 13,000 copies.

Through his book and teaching, Hammett formed a relationship with PGA Touring Pro, Kenny Knox. This led to his working for several years as a lead instructor at the Kenny Knox Golf Academy in Tallahassee, Florida. He continued teaching in Tallahassee as the director of instruction at Hilaman Park Golf Course for many years. During this time, Hammett was also part of a team that planted a church in Tallahassee. He helped build that church for 15 years and it continues to this day.

In conjunction with his golf ministry, Hammett has traveled and ministered in several venues, including clinics, lecture events and churches—taking his golf clubs to the pulpit to release Kingdom messages through the medium of the golf swing. He's even led the chapel service on the PGA Tour. And his ministry life hasn't just been limited to the golf world. He's also helped build and lead different churches and ministries for the last 25 years.

Hammett currently lives in Franklin, Tennessee with his beautiful wife and three children. He's on the teaching staff with Ben Pellicani and the Pelli Golf Programs at the Westhaven Golf Club. Chuck is also the head golf coach at Grace Christian Academy. With his wife Bobbi, the Hammetts also run their charity, The Angel Foundation. This is a prayer ministry that provides a beautiful angel blanket to children, adults and US Soldiers in challenging situations. Please visit **www.angelfoundation.me** to learn more. He also continues to serve local churches and ministries in the Nashville area.

Booking Information

All of Hammett's years of golf and ministry experience have culminated in his ministry, Kingdom Golf Connection. Hammett has an extraordinary ability to release powerful messages through golf clinics, speaking events and church meetings. Chuck Hammett connects to his audience, teaching them how to live life on this earth as intended from God' perspective. He thrives on revealing Kingdom truths and helping God's people understand who they are as true sons and daughters of the Most High. Through Kingdom Golf Connection, you can also take advantage of ministry golf events that Chuck puts on at some amazing golf resorts around the country. Through these events, you'll be ministered to through the game of golf during the day and receive deep ministry in worship, teaching and prayer in the evenings. These ministry golf events are great for church groups, pastoral staffs, families and corporate retreats. This is an amazing experience you'll not want to miss out on.

To learn more about the Kingdom Golf Connection ministry opportunities:

1. Watch this short video at www.vimeo.com/278997258
2. Connect with us on Face Book at Kingdom Golf Connection.

In order to book Chuck Hammett for an event with your church or ministry, contact him at info@kingdomgolfconnection.com.

Made in the USA
Columbia, SC
11 June 2020

10000870R00085